Learn Correct English

A Book of Grammar, Usage and Composition

Learn Correct English

A Book of Grammar, Usage and Composition

Professor Shiv K. Kumar

Retired, Professor of English,

Central University, Hyderabad

Dr Hemalatha Nagarajan

Reader, Central Institute of English and

Foreign Languages, Hyderabad

Pearson

The authors and publishers wish to thank Sonia Gandhi for permission to reprint the extract from Jawaharlal Nehru' s letter addressed to his daughter.

ISBN 978-81-317-0898-9

First Impression, 2007
Third Impression, 2011
Fourth Impression, 2012

Published by Pearson India Education Services Pvt. Ltd, CIN: U72200TN2005PTC057128

Head Office: 1st Floor, Berger Tower, Plot No. C-001A/2, Sector 16B, Noida – 201 301,Uttar Pradesh, India.

Registered Office: Featherlite, 'The Address' 5th Floor, Survey No 203/10B, 200 Ft MMRD Road, Zamin Pallavaram, Chennai - 600044
Website: in.pearson.com; Email:companysecretary.india@pearson.com

Digitally printed in India by Trinity Academy for Corporate Training Ltd, New Delhi in the year of 2025.

CONTENTS

PART 1: Grammar

8.	Silky **turns up** after nine months	Creating and extending meanings.	The use of phrasal verbs. The use of prepositional verbs.	**73**
9.	Reacting **immediately**	Expressing how/ when/why an action is performed.	The use of adverbs.	**79**
10.	It traveled **for** fifty-six years!	Indicating time, duration and place.	The use of prepositions.	**88**
11.	**Littering, spitting** and **honking**	Expressing likes, dislikes and hobbies	The use of gerunds.	**91**
12.	**On becoming intoxicated,** he thought....	Expressing time, reason, condition, means.	The use of participles.	**96**
13.	If you see the water recede quickly, **run** toward higher ground. . . If I **had** a holiday, I **would** go to the Arctic If she **had scolded** me, **I wouldn't have been** a thief	Talking about cause and effect or outcome of actions Talking about imaginary situations and their consequences. Describing impossible conditions.	The use of the open condition. The use of the possible and the improbable condition. The use of the impossible condition.	**104**
14.	The cat **asked** and the mouse **replied** **I instruct you to.....**	Reporting statements, commands and requests.	Reported speech (statements, commands, requests).	**115**
15.	**Their fate** only the UN can decide	How to highlight or emphasize something.	The use of inversion for focusing.	**124**

PART 2: Letter Writing

PART 3: Study Skills

INTRODUCTION

'Learn Correct English' is a book that aims to make you an **accurate** user of the English language. Most often there is a communication gap because we do not convey our ideas accurately. To make our thoughts and ideas clear, we need to use proper grammatical tools.

To make this point clear, let us examine this leave letter.
An employee applied for leave as follows: 'Since I have to go to my village to sell my land along with my wife, please sanction me one week leave.'

Do you think he wanted to sell his wife too? Of course, not! Yet, that is the message conveyed by this letter! The writer has used articles, prepositions, conjunctions, verbs and nouns rightly, and yet the message does not convey what it is intended to convey. The communication gap has been created due to improper/ inaccurate word order.

The main focus in this book is not on grammatical structures *per se* but on their functions and their use in speech and writing. Authentic materials have been used to highlight the grammatical points discussed in each unit. The common mistakes in the usage of these points have also been mentioned. We have included extensive examples of common errors. The approach adopted has been a mix of the traditional and the new communicative style. It cannot be denied that most books on grammar are loaded with academic jargon that makes the learning of a language dull and boring. Our main endeavour has been to move away from this and make it as enjoyable and useful for the learner as possible.

Apart from the grammatical points, the book also introduces the learner to the world of letters and study skills. It equips him/her with the skills to progress in the academic world.

We hope that the book will be useful for both undergraduate students in our universities and the general reader who wants to achieve competence in the correct usage of English.

TO THE TEACHER

We know that grammar is a tool for communication: it is a means to an end and not the end itself. The end is to make our learners **fluent and proficient users** of the language. Keeping this principle in mind, we expect you to:

- ✓ Relate grammatical rules to meaning
- ✓ Relate them to their contexts of use
- ✓ Focus on their use in real world contexts
- ✓ Supplement the materials with additional tasks if required (and if time permits!)
- ✓ Teach the rules to make learners understand how the language works without making them learn these by heart

We hope you find the book user-friendly. We would be glad to have your comments/ suggestions.

Shiv K. Kumar Hemalatha Nagarajan

PART 1

GRAMMAR

DELHI, AGRA AND JAIPUR

Learning to Name: Nouns

Pavan Kumar and his *wife, Sunanda*, stood on the *balcony* of their *house*, the *Rainbow*, looking at the *flowers* in their *garden — roses, lilies* and *jasmines*. Although they'd lived for short periods in *Kanpur, Mumbai* and *Delhi*, they had decided to live permanently in *Agra*. They liked the city for its *beauty, silence* and *elegance*. There was the *Taj Mahal*, just a couple of *miles* away, a *monument* to love.

If you read this passage closely, you will find several elements in it—the names of persons (Pavan Kumar and Sunanda), of places (like Agra, Mumbai, Kanpur and Delhi) and of things (like roses, lilies and jasmines).

We may think of some more names—John Smith, Sheila Ram, Kapil Srivastava. Or the name of places like Chandigarh, Nagpur or Chennai; or of things like a house, an apple or a rose. If we put these three elements together, they will make a noun. It should now be possible for us to define a noun as the name of a person, place or thing

Categories of Nouns

There are two principal classes of nouns—**Concrete and Abstract**. If you again look at the opening paragraph of this chapter, you will see such nouns as:

Pavan Kumar, Sunanda, balcony, house, lilies, roses, jasmines,
Kanpur, Mumbai, city, Taj Mahal, monument.

These are the names of persons (Sunanda), places (Kanpur, Mumbai) or things (roses, balcony and house). Because you can see or touch all these, they are called **Concrete Nouns**. They are visible and present physically.

Now look at such nouns in the same paragraph as:

beauty, silence and love

Since they cannot be touched or seen, they are called **Abstract Nouns**. They can only be felt or thought about—for instance, love, happiness, anger, philosophy, health, youth.

Now let us break **Concrete Nouns** into four smaller categories:

- **Proper Nouns**

Delhi, Nagpur, England, The Taj Mahal,
Parker (pen), Ambassador (car), Horlicks (milk)

Since these are names of things, places or persons, they are called Proper Nouns. Remember that each Proper Noun should begin with a capital letter (e.g. Akbar, Germany, Himalayas, Pond's (cream).

Note that the names of products like cars, milk, and pens are also proper nouns as these are 'special' names given by their companies.

- **Common Nouns**

Look at the following names:

queen, servant, flower, wall, table, spoon, tray, cap, valley

Since these names are used to describe any one of a group of things, persons or places, they are called Common Nouns.

(Note : But there are few Proper Nouns which may take the form of Common Nouns.)

Ram is a Tarzan	(a strong person)
Kalidasa is the Shakespeare of India.	(the literary genius)
He is a Kumbhakaran	(someone who sleeps most of the time)
He is the Hamlet in our family	(someone always lost in thought)
He is the Everest amongst writers	(the most eminent)

We generally use 'a/an ———' when there is no phrase after the noun.
He is a Tarzan.

If there is a phrase that tells us more about the noun, then we use 'the————'
He is the Shakespeare of India.

- **Collective Nouns**

Look at the following:

a *herd* of elephants
a *complex* of apartments
a *procession* of labourers
a *caravan* of camels
a *cluster* of bushes
a *galaxy* of film stars

Since the italicized words, listed above, describe names of groups, they are called Collective Nouns—i.e., names collected into a group.

Ordinarily, a Collective Noun is used as a singular—a herd, a team, a committee. But if there is a division in a group, it is used as a plural, and it takes a plural verb. For instance, if there is a difference of judgement in a judicial bench, we'll say : The bench have agreed to dismiss the petition.

Note the following examples of Collective Nouns used as plural:

The *staff* were divided in their decision to postpone examinations.
The *union* were divided on the date to begin their strike.
The *committee* were unable to agree in the selection of a suitable candidate.

(There are, however, a few Collective Nouns that are never used as singular, they always carry the plural form. For instance: *people*, *cattle*)

- **Material Nouns**

A material noun refers to such objects as are made out of matter. For instance:

stone, brick, silk, steel, wood, silver

In certain cases, Material Nouns take the form of Common Nouns—such as:

i. A bomb blast was reported in today's *paper*.
Will you give me a ream of *paper*?

ii. This vase is made of *glass*.
Please pass on that *glass* of milk to me.

iii. The Taj Mahal is made of *marble*.
My sister enjoys playing with *marbles*.

iv. This carpet is made of *wool*.
Maya is holding a ball of *wool* in her hand.

Common Mistakes in the Use of Nouns

(a) There are some nouns which are always used in their singular forms — such as :

weather, advice, news, furniture, luggage, information, pleasure, noise

Incorrect : Don't make a noise in class.
Correct : Don't make noise in class.

(since *noise*, like *pleasure*, or *nonsense* or *rubbish*, cannot be counted, it should not be preceded by the indefinite article *a*.)

Incorrect : I have a great pleasure in writing few words about you.
Correct : I have great pleasure in writing few words about you.

Incorrect : What a nonsense to think of playing cricket in the rain!
Correct : What nonsense to think of playing cricket in the rain!

Incorrect : I have given you an advices in this matter.
Correct : I have given you a piece of advice in this matter.

(Also, never say *advices* which means *information*)

Incorrect : The hunter killed a lot of deers in the forest.
Correct : The hunter killed a lot of deer in the forest.

(b) Given below are nouns which are always used in the plural :

trousers, tongs, scissors, thanks, police, pliers, riches and shears

Incorrect : Please get me a scissor to cut this paper.
Correct : Please get me a pair of scissors to cut the paper.

Incorrect : Please give me a tong to hold the nail.
Correct : Please get me a pair of tongs to hold the nail.

(so we say a pair of shears, a pair of compasses, a pair of spectacles, and so on.)

(Please remember that the singular of 'police' is 'a police man'.)

- **Compound Nouns**

Don't make wrong plurals in such cases as given below :

ladies-doctors, mothers-in-laws and houses-maids

The correct usage is *lady-doctors, mothers-in-law and house-maids*

- **Collective Nouns**

These nouns can be used both in the singular or plural form, depending upon the situation. When, for example, a team is taken as a unit, it will be treated a singular.

Incorrect : The cricket team are having their breakfast.
Correct : The cricket team is having its breakfast.

Our cricket team have been trained by John Wright. (meaning, every member of the team has been trained by John Wright.)

- **Possessive case of Nouns**

i. Remember that there are exceptions to the general rule that a possessive case may be used only with nouns denoting living objects.

Incorrect : His bungalow's number is given to the left of the front gate.
Correct : The number of his bungalow is given to the left of the front door.

Given below are some exceptions

The moon's beams, the sun's rays, a stone's throw, a rupee's worth, a week's picnic, out of harm's way, in my mind's eye, for goodness' sake, at my fingers' tips and for form's sake.

ii. Sometimes, the extra's' after names already ending in 's' are dropped—if they sound unusual.

John Keats' poem, on Zeus' strength, or Srinivas' good qualities.

iii. Remember that there are adjectives used as nouns, which should not take the 's' even if they are applied to persons.

Incorrect : The rich's failings are often ignored.
Correct : The failings of the rich are often ignored.

iv. In case of group names, it is the second name that takes the possessive form if the noun they refer to belongs to both.

(e.g. 'children' in the example given below)

Incorrect : Ram's and Sita's children are also leading characters in *The Ramayana*.
Correct : Ram and Sita's children are also leading characters in *The Ramayana*.

Incorrect : Kalidas and Bharati's poetry.
Correct : Kalidas' and Bharati's poetry.

TASK 1

Correct the following.

1. I can imagine the flowers in his garden in the eye of my mind.

   ----

2. My sister is of course is my father's and my mother's daughter.

   ----

3. The gang of robbers were arrested by the police who were hiding behind the wall.

   ----

4. Charles's and Mary Lamb's *Tales from Shakespeare* are very interesting.

   ----

5. Since it is a good weather, let us play cricket.

   ----

6. Bring me my trouser, please.

   ----

7. I have a great pleasure in recommending Ram Kishen for the job.

   ----

8. He was at the end of his wits when he saw a snake.

   ----

9. For the sake of goodness don't harass me.

   ----

10. Their mothers-in-laws are always fighting with each other.

TASK 2

Rewrite these sentences using collective nouns. Use any of the words given in this list. (Don't forget to make the verb singular where necessary.)

pack team staff herd range swarm stack gang crew bunch

1. My friend gave me <u>ten or eleven beautiful lilies</u>.

   ----

2. The people who work in this software company have flexible timings.

3. When you go to Tirumala, you will see seven mountains in a row.

4. The people who work for the airline were well dressed.

5. My daughter gave me the fifty two cards and asked me to perform a trick.

6. During vacation time, most schools keep the tables and chairs on top of one another in the corner of the classroom.

7. Some five of six thieves entered the jewellery shop and stole the ornaments.

8. Krishna found it difficult to get the large number of sheep that had escaped from the field.

9. The Government has appointed a group of scientists to study the causes of pollution in the cities.

10. Hundreds of bees entered the house when the windows were opened.

TASK 3

Fill in the blanks with the form of the noun in parentheses that is appropriate to the grammatical context of the sentence and the meaning of the passage as a whole.

DON'T REUSE WATER BOTTLES

You may think you're helping the ——————————(environment/environments) when you reuse water ————————(bottle/bottles), but researchers say it could cause —————— ———(damage/ damages) to your health. Dangerous ————————(bacteria/ bacterias) and potentially toxic plastic ——————————(compound/compounds) have been found in the water bottles typically reused in ——————————(classroom/classrooms) and —— ——————————(workplace/workplaces).

A study of ———————— (kid's/ kids') water ————————(bottle/ bottles) in a Canadian school found bacterial ———————————— (contamination/ contaminations) in about a third of the ————————————(sample/ samples) collected. The bacteria probably came from the ———————(children's/ childrens') hands and mouths over ——————(time/ times) as they repeatedly used the same bottles , without washing them or allowing them to dry.

An American ——————(study/studies) suggests that the kind of thorough ——————— (washing/ washings) that could kill bacteria might speed up the breakdown of the ———— ——(plastic/ plastics).

TASK 4

Learning to use the right nouns.

Given below is a news report. Hari accidentally dropped some ink on it and some words are missing. Use appropriate nouns (from the list given below) to fill in the blanks to convey the right meaning.

limitations	stamina	showing	pitfalls	trouble	stead
drive	importance	season	track	potential	consistency

Narain Karthikeyan of Jordan F1 had an excellent drive at Sepang F1 2005, staying out of ——————— and driving a strong and consistent race. Narain knew his and his car's — ——————, and drove sensibly. With the Sepang ————— being extremely hard on the drivers, tyres and cars, ——————— and ——————— was of paramount ——— ————— and Narain presented a brilliant ——————— avoiding any of the ———— — that dogged others.

If one goes by the last two races, Narain sure looks like he has great ———————— and such a —————— will stand him in good ——————— through the rest of the ———— ———— and perhaps into the 2006 F1 season.

SIGNALLING A NOUN: ARTICLES

Ram: Aren't beggars a nuisance? One sees them everywhere—on **the** road, in front of **a** temple, **a** church or **a** mosque, anywhere, anytime.

Shyam: Indeed, they are omnipresent. Remember, **the** other day we saw **a** cripple near **a** gas station—**a** middle-aged woman, wearing **a** tattered sari and carrying **a** two-month-old child in her arms?

Ram: Yes. I do remember. Wasn't she **the** one who wore **a** pair of green slippers?

Shyam: Well, **a** couple of days later, I saw her running across **the** traffic lights to catch **a** passerby.

Ram: How adept these beggars are at feigning to be **a** cripple, **a** deaf or **a** dumb creature.

Shyam: Not only that. They can exploit your religious sentiments. **A** week ago, I saw **a** beggar holding **a** copy of **the** Bhagwad Gita in his hand. **A** rupee, sir, he said, in **the** name of Lord Krishna!

Ram: I can imagine another beggar using **the** Bible or **the** Granth Sahib to get alms.

Shyam: But if you wish to see them in hordes, you should visit Allahabad. There they swarm like flies on **the** banks of the Ganages or **the** Jamuna. They wouldn't let go **a** devotee unless he parts with **a** rupee or **a** fiver.

Ram: Even in Hyderabad, you see them lazing along the bank of **the** Musi river every evening after they've picked up **a** bowlful of coins and currency notes.

Shyam: I have **an** uncle in **the** Police Department who tells me that some beggars even own two-room houses on **the** outskirts of **the** city. You may even see **a** beggar riding **a** scooter or **a** motorcycle.

Ram: Amazing!

Shyam: Only this morning, I saw **a** beggar near **a** fruit vendor. He put out his hand to **a** customer and said, in **a** pleading tone: 'Please, sir, buy me **an** orange or **an** apple. God will bless you.'

Ram: Imagine **the** audacity of this man. But I was once confronted by **a** lean, tall fellow who pushed into my hands **a** framed certificate which read: 'I am deaf and dumb. My father is dying. He was injured in **a** road accident. Please help.'

But when I just walked away, I heard **the** man shouting to **a** fellow beggar. Pointing at me, they were both giggling.

Shyam: It is **a** thousand pities that our government cannot do anything about this social menace.

The words in bold i.e. **a, an** and **the** are known as **articles.** They signal the coming of a noun. '**A**' and '**an**' are indefinite articles as they can usually refer to any member of a group. '**The**' is a definite article as it refers to a specific member of a group.

- **Indefinite article:**

They are used with singular nouns with no definite reference.

a temple, **a** church, **a** mosque, **a** cripple, **a** gas station, **a** beggar . . . (any one)

With the corresponding plural nouns, we use '**some**'

some beggars, **some** gas stations, **some** passersby . . .

- **Definite article:**

The definite article '**the**' is used with singular and plural nouns that refer to specific or particular members of a group.

The man (which man? The man who pretended to be deaf and dumb)

The beggar (which beggar? The one in green slippers)

The definite article is used:

i. with the names of rivers: **The Ganges, the Jamuna,**

ii. with the names of deserts, forests, gulfs: **The Sahara, The Persian Gulf**

iii. with uncountable nouns: My daughter refused to drink **the** milk. (I gave my daughter a glass of milk: as 'glass' can be counted, we use 'a' here)

iv. with a noun that has already been introduced.
I saw a beggar in the market. **The** beggar was pretending to be dumb.

v. with 'generic' nouns i,e. nouns that belong to the whole class.
The tiger is a ferocious animal. (all tigers)

vi. with superlatives (**the** hottest months, **the** first prize)

- **No article:**

No article is required when:

i. the noun is non-countable and it is used in a general sense.

Water is a rare commodity in our city. So we should not waste it.

Honesty is the best policy, but fraud seems to be the best policy nowadays!

However, when these nouns are made specific by a qualifying phrase after them then 'the' is used.

The water in the bottle is dirty. Don't drink it.

The honesty of the young boy touched us.

ii. the noun is the name of a country (except **the** Netherlands and **the** United States of America)

iii. the noun is a name of an island, continent, lake, mountain or a street

iv. the noun is a name of a language (Telugu, Hindi, Bangla)

v. the noun is a name of a sport (cricket, hockey, carom)

vi. the noun is a name of a subject (science, history, geography)

TASK 1

Complete the sentences with a suitable article.

1. Monsieur Eiffel is considered a / an / the / no article needed father of modern steel construction.

2. He was born of a / an / the / no article needed prosperous family in France in 1832.

3. He graduated from a / an / the / no article needed Central School of Engineering in Paris.

4. He then went on to work for a / an / the / no article needed railway construction company.

5. Eiffel built a / an / the / no article needed first wind tunnel that could be used.

6. He built some of a / an / the / no article needed world's biggest bridges.

7. His daring methods have revolutionized a / an / the / no article needed bridge design.

8. A / An / The / no article needed Eiffel Tower was built by him.

9. Almost a million visitors to [a / an / the / no article needed] Paris every summer climb [a / an / the / no article needed] tower to look down at [a / an / the / no article needed] city.

10. For many people [a / an / the / no article needed] impression of that view lasts [a / an / the / no article needed] lifetime.

TASK 2

Correct the errors (if any) in the use of articles in the following sentences.

1. Prior to a election, the candidate is addressing a group of the farmers in the rural region.
   'Let me assure you that in addition to my other promises, should you vote for me, I will guarantee you the new bridge.'
   'But we don't have_ river!' the farmer yelled out.
   'Then I promise you an river,' a candidate replied

2. Walking into his shop, the chemist finds the customer leaning heavily against _ wall.
   'What's wrong with that man?' he asks his assistant.
   'Well,' an assistant replies.
   'He came in this morning to get something for his cough. I couldn't find _ cough syrup, so I gave him a entire bottle of laxative.'
   'You can't treat the cough with the laxatives!' shouted a chemist.
   'Yes, you can. Now, he is afraid to cough.'

TASK 3

Fill in the blanks with appropriate articles.

1. ________five –year-old boy had one line in ______kindergarten Christmas play, appearing in __________angel's robes to say: 'I bring you good tidings!'

After ________rehearsal, _________boy aked his mother what 'tidings' was. She explained that tidings meant news.

Came ___________performance and he became flustered. After ________long embarrassing silence, he blurted out: 'Hey, I've got news for you!'

2. __________railway station at Paris was crowded with tourists. _________French make travel by train ________gay occasion, full of confusion, colour and laughter. At _________barrier, my daughter made ____________unsuccessful attempt to find our tickets. ________ticket collector looked at us, loaded with luggage, and smilingly waved us on.

3. I installed ________night light in _____shell I found on ________beach. My wife took ________instant dislike to it, and at _______next garage sale it was ________first thing she put out.

I was happy when ________woman kept coming back to check it out and then finally bought it. 'That will look great in your house.' I said.

'Oh, it's not for me,' she said, 'My ladies' club is having _________sale and we were asked to bring _____ most hideous thing we can find. What I've got is __________winner!'

2

THEY THINK **WE** HAVE HIDDEN GOD!

Personal and Possessive Pronouns

Read the following:

God is missing!

Ram and Shyam were brothers who were always up to some mischief. Several times **they** were pulled up for little thefts in the house—a fountain pen, a knife or a packet of biscuits. So troubled were **their** parents for **their** misconduct that **they** threatened to call the police and have **them** put behind bars. But even **this** threat didn't work. Then **their** father decided to take **them** over to the family priest, hoping that **he**'d be able to put some fear of God into **their** hearts.

So, the following day, both brothers found themselves at the temple, standing in front of Pandit Prabhu Dayal. The priest decided to talk to each of **them** separately. So while **he** sent Shyam out in the courtyard, **he** held back Ram for his questioning.

'Where is God?' the priest asked **him**, sternly.

When there was no response from Ram, **he** repeated **his** question twice: 'Where is God?'

Ram looked scared, **his** face went pale. Then suddenly, **he** bolted away. Outside the temple stood **his** younger brother Shyam, waiting in suspense.

Ram pulled **his** brother by the arm and whispered into **his** ears:

'Let's run away. **This** time **it** is God that is missing and they think **we** are responsible for **it!'**

Who does 'they' 'we' and 'it' refer to in the sentence:

'They think **we** are responsible for **it.'**

'They' is used to refer to most people in the village (which includes the priest, of course).

'We' refers to the two brothers and 'it' refers to God missing.

They, it and **we** are personal pronouns. Instead of naming a person, place or thing, we can use a pronoun to refer to them.

Pronouns are short substitutes for nouns or for groups of words.

Talk to *the man in the red shirt*.. ~~*The man in the red shirt*~~ He will know what to do. ~~*The person listening to me*~~ You will learn a lot from ~~*the man in the red shirt*~~ **him.** ~~*All people*~~ **Everybody** will agree with ~~*the person talking*~~ **me.**

- **Personal pronouns** refer to specific people or things.

	Subject forms		Object forms		Possessive forms	
	singular	*plural*	*singular*	*plural*	*singular*	*plural*
1st person	I	we	me	us	my / mine	our / ours
2nd person	you	you	you	you	your / yours	your / yours
3rd person	he	they	him	them	his	their / theirs
	she	they	her	them	her / hers	their / theirs
	it	they	it	them	its	their / theirs

Making pronouns refer clearly to something

A pronoun usually refers back to some noun or a group of words in a sentence.

Read the following sentence:

When a baby has finished drinking milk from its bottle, you should unscrew its head. You should then rinse **it** thoroughly under the tap, and put **it** away in a cool place.

Does the pronoun **'it'** refer to the baby or the bottle?

How can you improve this sentence to avoid confusion?

When a baby has finished drinking milk from its bottle, you should unscrew the **bottle's head.** You should then rinse **it** thoroughly under the tap, and put **it** away in a cool place.

So be careful when you use pronouns next time.

TASK 1

Rewrite the following sentences to make the meaning clear.

1. If the milk is kept in the fridge too long, it will get spoilt.

   ----

2. When Renu ran with the whistle in her mouth, she was losing breath. So she soon stopped **it.**

   ----

3. People normally do not like summer for it heats the walls and makes **them** crack.

   ----

4. Before Rita went near her kitten, **she** was meowing excitedly. **She** tickled her face and then **she** picked **her** up and went in **her** car.

   ----

5. Ram and Shyam were friends of Prema. **He** did not like **him** and so fought with **him.**

TASK 2

Say clearly who or what the underlined pronouns refer to. Rewrite some of the sentences to make the meaning clear.

NEIGHBOURLY CONCERN

Robin Rao was travelling by air for the first time and because of **it**, **he** was tense and nervous. Halfway through the flight, **his** stomach turned over and **he** threw up all over his neighbour, a huge African wrestler. **He** was asleep but what would happen to **him** when **he** awoke? His stomach started churning again.

Suddenly **he** awoke. He stared with disbelief at the mess in **his** lap. He turned towards his neighbour. His heart leaped—and then immediately **he** got a brainwave: 'Rough wasn't it?' he said with neighbourly concern. 'I hope **you're** feeling better now.'

(Check your passage with the correct version given below.)

Robin Rao was traveling by air for the first time and because of it, he was tense and nervous. Halfway through the flight, his stomach turned over and he threw up all over his neighbour, a huge African wrestler. The wrestler was asleep but what would happen to Rao when he awoke? Rao's stomach started churning again.

Suddenly, the wrestler awoke. He stared with disbelief at the mess in his lap. He turned towards his neighbour. Rao's heart leaped—and then immediately, he got a brainwave: 'Rough wasn't it?' he said with neighbourly concern. 'I hope you're feeling better now.'

A personal pronoun must agree with the noun or the words it refers to.

The *students in my class* will need **their** course book soon.

Meera doesn't seem to want **her** book, though.

In the first sentence above, the pronoun, **their**, is plural because the words it refers to, The *students in my class,* is plural. In the second sentence, **her** is singular because what it refers to, *Meera,* is singular. When the pronoun and the word or the words it refers to match in this way, we say they 'agree'.

1. If we mix up the usage of person in a sentence, things can get very confusing for the reader.

*When **they** came out, **you** could see everything had gone wrong.*

This sentence is awkward because we move here from third person to second person.

2. You should also make sure that the pronoun agrees with the noun it refers to in number.

*I have to meet my **student** before **they** leave the class.*

The sentence refers to just one student, and yet the use of the pronoun 'they' implies more than one. Therefore, the pronoun does not agree with the noun it refers to in number.

Incorrect	:	The cricket players will need to bring his own kit to the stadium.
Correct	:	The cricket players will need to bring their own kit to the stadium.
Incorrect	:	While they barked, you knew a thief had entered the house.
Correct	:	While the dogs barked, you knew a thief had entered the house.
Incorrect	:	The teacher wanted to meet her students before she left (the teacher?).
Correct	:	The teacher wanted to see her students before they left (the students).

TASK 3

Develop the following clues into a story. Use pronouns correctly instead of nouns wherever necessary. Give it a suitable title. Check if they 'agree' with the noun or words they refer to.

Robert Bruce — Scottish leader was fighting to free Scotland from English rule — was defeated in battle once — sought refuge in a cave. Was sad and disheartened. Saw a spider — was trying to climb its web — six times spider tried — but failed — finally on the seventh attempt — spider succeeded. Bruce inspired by spider's determination — Bruce decided to carry on the fight. Within seven years — Bruce master of Scotland.

TASK 4

Read the following advertisement:

Wanted a Software Professional for a Multinational Company

Wanted software professional. He should be well versed in C, C++, Java and Oracle. He will work on short term projects. He should have a degree in Engineering with two to three years of experience. An attractive salary can be considered for the right man.

Use of gender-neutral pronouns

Nowadays, there is a tendency to use a more neutral form of nouns and pronouns. We use terms like 'chairperson' instead of 'chairman' and 'flight attendant' instead of 'air hostess'. The word 'actor' is used to refer to a man as well as a woman who acts.

In English, the pronoun 'he' is normally used to refer to an entire class of people. However, we now use other gender-neutral forms.

For instance, the sentence

'If anyone wants a job, **he** can apply for it.'

can be rewritten in the following ways:

1. Use the plural.

'If anyone wants a job, **they** can apply for it.'

2. Replace the masculine pronoun with ONE or YOU

'If anyone wants a job, **one** can apply for it.'

'If anyone wants a job, **you** can apply for it.'

3. Use HE OR SHE

'If anyone wants a job, **he/ she** can apply for it.'

Can you change the pronouns and nouns (if necessary) in the advertisement given above into their more neutral form? Rewrite the advertisement below with the necessary changes.

A **MEMORABLE** OCCASION

Describe Well: Adjectives

Read the following passage.

Since Ravindran had just turned twenty-one, his father, a steel industrialist, decided to let him have a gala birthday party. This should be a *memorable* occasion for his son. In the guava and mango trees bordering the *vast*, *luscious* lawn of his *spacious* bungalow, blinked *multi-coloured* bulbs, like stars twinkling in the *blue* sky on a *pleasant*, *spring* evening. All along the compound wall were arranged *large* tables loaded with a variety of *Chinese*, *North* and *South Indian* dishes so that each guest may have the food of his choice. There was *enough* food for a *thousand* guests.

Although Ravindran had invited *all* his college mates, he hoped that George, his *closest* friend, would be the *first* to arrive. But when he did not show up until seven, Ravindran wore an *anxious* look. 'What kind of a friend is George?' he said to himself. 'Not *thoughtful* enough to come *early*.' He continued to help Sita, his *younger* sister, in supervising the arrangements.

In a corner of the lawn was placed a huge stereo-system with *two mammoth* speakers to entertain the guests. Ravindran's father had also commissioned Hamid Khan, a *renowned* ghazal singer as the *top* attraction of the evening.

Among the *distinguished* guests invited were a *former* Chief Justice, and *a few* ministers of the State Cabinet.

Read the above passage carefully. All the words italicized in this passage are called adjectives. An adjective may be defined as a word that qualifies a noun—the name of a person, place or thing. All these adjectives may be classified in different categories—numerical, quantitative, descriptive, demonstrative, distributive, etc. Let us now understand each category separately.

Categories of Adjectives

- **Numerical Adjectives**

These are adjectives that refer to numbers—of things, persons or places. Note, for instance, the sentence in the above passage : '. . . food for a *thousand* guests.' There are also some other numerical adjectives in this passage e.g. 'Although Ravindran had invited *all* his college mates . . .' Also, note the sentences : '. . . and *a few* ministers . . .,' 'He hoped that George . . . would be the *first* to arrive.'

Given below are some more examples :

i. *No* non-vegetarian dishes were served at the party.

ii. There are always *some* guests who arrive late at parties.

iii. *Most* people love flattery.

iv. Latif was the *last* to board the bus.

You may have noticed that although such numericals as *all*, *some*, *many*, *several*, *none*, do not specify any precise number, they also suggest numbers.

On the other hand, although there are adjectives which suggest a precise number, they assume a different form:

We receive our salary on the *first* of every month. (e.g. *fourth*, *fifth*, *sixth*, etc.)

- **Descriptive/Qualitative Adjectives**

These are adjectives that show the kind, quality or condition of the nouns they qualify.

Read the following sentences:

i. The *Russian* Prime Minister is arriving in Delhi tomorrow.

ii. He is an *American* actor.

iii. Saul Bellow is a *Jewish* author.

iv. B.K. Das is a *talented* speaker.

v. The bed-sheet is *grey*.

vi. A *terrified* look appeared on his face as he saw a policeman at his door.

vii. He lives in a *multi-storey* apartment.

viii. He drives a *Toyota* car.

Note that although *Russian* Prime Minister, *American* actor or *Jewish* author are formed from Proper Nouns, they should still be treated as adjectives of quality.

There is another category of adjectives of quality which are based on the Past and Present Participial of verbs :

a. Present Participial

i. My neighbour has very *pleasing* manners.
ii. The Headmistress of the school has a very *forbidding* look.

iii. This boy has a very *smiling* face.

iv. May I have your *visiting* card, please?

b. Past Participial

i. Shyam had a *worried* look.

ii. I had an *unexpected* visit from an old friend.

iii. His *fractured* shoulder needs immediate surgery.

iv. The *wounded* soldier was carried away on a stretcher.

v. The *defeated* politician was now friendless.

vi. The *divorced* woman is feeling very lonely.

- **Interrogative Adjective**

i. *What* sort of friend was George?

ii. *Whose* car is this?

iii. *Which* road leads to the Krishna temple?

When *what*, *whose*, *which* appear with nouns to qualify them, they are called Interrogative Adjectives.

- **Distributive Adjective**

Read the following sentence.

i. *Each* guest may have the food of his choice.

ii. England expects *every* man to do his duty, said Nelson.

iii. He has to go to work *every* day including Sundays.

iv. Ram can type with *either* hand.

v. The diplomat was with *neither* side.

A Distributive Adjective points to either one of the two, or more things or persons—which may be taken individually or in separate groups.

Note the difference between the usage of *each* and *every*. *Each* stresses the individual, and not a group, whereas *every* is used for *all* of a group (of more than two) though considered single.

But, remember, that all these Distributive Adjectives (*each*, *every*, *either* and *neither*) carry singular verbs after them because those words belong to the Singular Number.

- **Demonstrative Adjective**

Read the following sentences:

i. *Such* friends should be avoided.

ii. *These* songs are very moving.

iii. *This* car is costlier than *that*.

You may notice that such adjectives as *this*, *that*, *such* point towards a person or persons (*friends*), thing (*car*) or things (*songs*). These adjectives are Demonstrative, because they demonstrate or show some quality in a noun.

- **Adjectives Showing Quantities or Quantifiers**

Such adjectives show how much, or how little, of something is intended.

Read the following sentences:

i. *Half* a glass of milk is enough for me.

ii. The court ordered the tenant to pay the *entire* amount of rental arrears.

iii. Since there was a strike in town I could not get *any* vegetables.

iv. Your words make *no* sense.

v. Will you pass on *some* sugar to me, please?

vi. I don't have *much* time to spend with you.

vii. A word of kindness is *enough* for me.

viii. A *little* discount in price is all I expect from you.

There are some adjectives which are sometimes used with nouns that are not countable:

i. Is there *any* cooking gas in the kitchen?

ii. *All* the provisions have been exhausted.

iii. My brother could have left *some* money for me.

iv. Before I reached the grocery store, *all* the wheat had been sold out.

Read the following.

When the Indian subcontinent was partitioned into two separate countries, Pakistan and India, countless refugees were forced to migrate from one side to another. The Hindus crossed from Pakistan into India, the Muslims fled from India to Pakistan.

But while both communities lost **most** members of their families in this exodus, **a lot of** horses and mules, which carried their scanty belongings, also perished. Among those killed, were **many** children who couldn't understand why their elders were killing each other. Since there were only **a few** soldiers on the highways, hardly **anyone** survived. **The few** who were fortunate enough to reach their destinations found themselves without food or shelter.

The words **some, many, most, a few, few, a lot of** are adjectives of quantity (also called quantifiers).

Such adjectives show how much, or how little, of something intended.

Read the following sentence:

i. *Half* a glass of milk is enough for me.

ii. The court ordered the tenant to pay the *entire* amount of rental arrears.

iii. Since there was a strike in town I could not get *any* vegetables.

iv. Your words make *no* sense.

v. Will you pass on *some* sugar to me, please?

vi. I don't have *much* time to spend with you.

vii. A word of kindness is *enough* for me.

viii. A *little* discount in price is all I expect from you.

Countable nouns	**Uncountable nouns**
all every	all
most..........>	most
many...........>	much
some.............>	some
a few................>	a little
few.......................>	.........> little

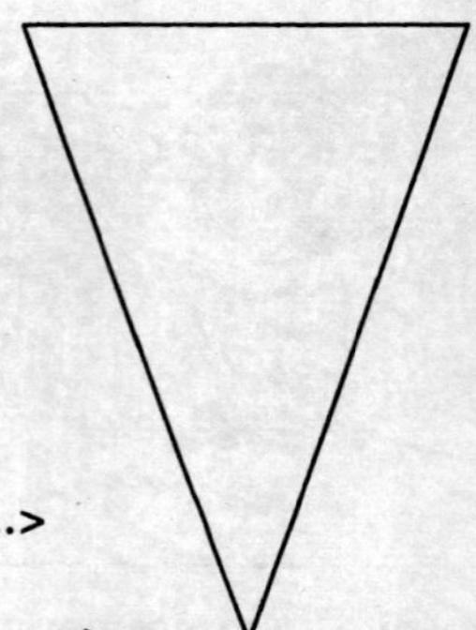

no(ne)

All/every, most, many, some, a few, few and no(ne) are quantifiers which are used with countable nouns (dogs, friends, cars). With uncountable nouns (money, advice, water, information), **all, most, much, some, a little, and no(ne)** are used.

'How much' and **'How many'** are used in negative sentences and in questions.

I don't have **much money** in my purse.

I don't have **many coins** in my purse.

How **much money** do you have in your purse?

How **many books** by Tagore have you read?

In positive statements, we use 'a lot of'.

I have **a lot of** money in my purse.

I have **a lot of** books in my bag.

'Some' is used in positive statements to indicate indefinite quantity and **'any'** is used in negative statements.

I have **some money** in my purse.

I have **some books** in my bag.

I don't have **any money** in my purse.

I don't have **any books** in my bag.

'A little' and **'a few'** have a positive meaning whereas **'little'** and **'few'** have a negative meaning.

I have **a little milk** at home to make a cup of coffee. (at least some)

I have **little milk** at home to make a cup of coffee. (hardly any)

There are **a few books** on Tagore in our library. (at least some)

There are **few books** on Tagore in our library. (hardly any)

'Enough' is used to talk of sufficient quantity of some noun.(countable/ uncountable)

I have **enough money** in my purse. I don't have to get money from the bank.

Our library has **enough books** on Tagore. You don't have to search elsewhere.

The quantifiers 'many' and 'much' can be graded as shown below.

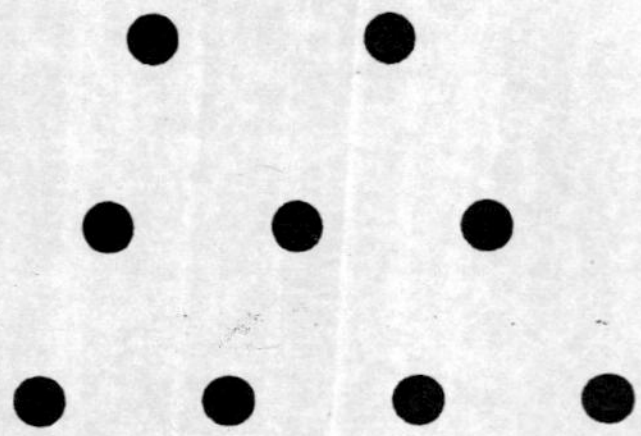

Many/ Much

More/ More

Most/ Most

The same is true of 'little' and 'few'.

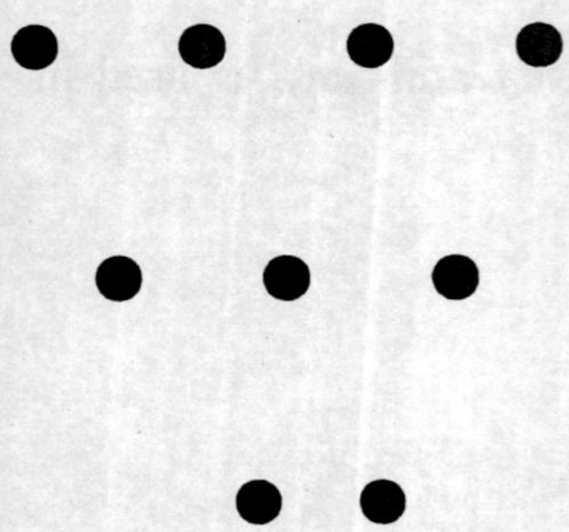

Little/ few

Less/ fewer

Least/ fewest

There are **many books** on Tagore at home, **more** in our library, but **most** in Shanti Niketan.

Much advice is given to students by their friends, **more** by their teachers and **most** by their parents.

Few people are millionaires, **fewer** are billionaires and **fewest** are multi –millionaires!

There was **little water** in the rivers, **less** in the lakes and **least** in the ponds.

Only with uncountable nouns	**With uncountable and countable nouns**	**Only with countable nouns**
How much?	How much? or How many?	How many?
a little	no/none	a few
a bit (of)	not any	a number (of)
-	some (any)	several
a great deal of	a lot of	a large number of
a large amount of	plenty of	a great number of
-	lots of	-
	+ noun	

TASK 1

*Look at the three advertisements given below and write a paragraph. Compare these three cars using quantifiers like **most, more, a little***

A	B	C
cost = 4 lakhs	cost = 6 lakhs	cost = 2 lakhs
mileage = 60 kmph	mileage = 80 kmph	mileage = 50 kmph
engine capacity=800cc	engine capacity=1000cc	engine capacity=900cc

TASK 2

Fill in the blanks with the right quantifier from the list given below.

① Some
② A little
③ Plenty
④ A few

⑤ Much of
⑥ Many
⑦ A lot of
⑧ A lot
⑨ Several of
⑩ Enough

The tsunami or the giant waves hit Chennai on the 26 December 2004.

There were ____________ people taking a walk on the beach.

________________ of them were walking close to the shore.

____________________ them were caught unawares.

There wasn't ________________ time for them to run away.

____________________ them were washed away.

________________ lucky ones held on to trees and survived.

Help came from ________________ sources. Food and clothes were gathered and sent to those affected by the tsunami.

________________ the food sent to Nicobar got spoilt as it could not reach them on time.

We hope that India has a tsunami warning system so that there is ——————warning before it strikes.

TASK 3

Mr. and Mrs. Kumar are moving into a new house. They are discussing what they would like to buy for it. Complete their dialogue by inserting an appropriate quantifier.

Mr. Kumar : I think we should get _________ new furniture for the house.

Mrs. Kumar : Yes we have _________ cane chairs but _________ decent sofa set. But of course, we don't have _________ space in the new house.

Mr. Kumar : Besides the furniture, we have to buy _________ fans and tubelights too.

Mrs. Kumar : Yes, _________ of our old tubelights aren't working. How about a new gas stove for my kitchen? There is a sale now.

Mr. Kumar : _________ gas stoves bought in sales last for more than a month.

Mrs. Kumar : You have ________ words of praise for whether I buy!

Mr. Kumar : And you have________ respect for me. Rahul, their son, enters the room.

Rahul : Firstly, promise me that there will be _______ quarrels in the new house.

TASK 4

Imagine you are the class Teacher of Class X. You are preparing the report card of Kiran. You are looking at his progress. Use quantifiers to describe his progress.

e.g. Kiran has made **some** progress in Math. His errors are **fewer**.

TASK 5

Make a survey of the television programmes that are watched by your classmates. Write a paragraph about the programme watched by

(1) most / many (2) some (3) a few (4) few (5) none of them.

Comparative Adjectives

WHO IS STRONGER?

Read the following fable:

> One day there was a quarrel between the wind and the sun as to which was the **stronger** of the two. They decided that whichever of them made a traveller take off his tunic should be considered **more powerful**.
>
> The wind began the contest. He blew, blew and blew, cold and fierce like a storm on the mountain top. The more he blew the closer the traveller wrapped his tunic around him.
>
> Then the sun arose. With his first rays he dispersed the mist and the cold.
>
> The traveller felt the warmth and smiled.
>
> But the sun shone **brighter** and brighter.
>
> The traveller was overcome with the heat. He took off his tunic and sat down to rest under a tree.
>
> The sun was declared the winner of the contest.

When we compare a particular quality in two nouns, we usually use the comparative suffix -er

strong — stronger
bright — brighter

However, if the adjective is a longer word (more than two syllables), we use 'more'

powerful — more powerful
beautiful — more beautiful

There are some adjectives with a different form in the comparative

good — better — best
little — less — least
bad — worse — worst
far — farther / further — farthest

up	upper	uppermost
in	inner	innermost (inner)
hind	hinder	hindmost (utmost)
out	outer	outermost
much, many	more	most

There are some adjectives with two syllables, and others with more than two syllables. Such adjectives are formed with *more* and *most* to suggest comparative and superlative degrees.

Note the following formations:

glorious	more glorious	most glorious
truthful	more truthful	most truthful
difficult	more difficult	most difficult
disgraceful	more disgraceful	most disgraceful
comfortable	more comfortable	most comfortable

Remember that these are sentences that do not suggest any comparison. Such sentences do not take a Definite Article before them:

i. This is *most* deplorable.

ii. It was a *most* painful spectacle.

iii. This is *most* unbearable.

iv. This is *most* enjoyable.

Adjectives often Incorrectly Used

There is a class of adjectives frequently misunderstood. It is, therefore, necessary to properly understand their correct usage.

a. *Less, Lesser*

(i) *Less* means smaller in duration, measurement or size. It is followed by *than*.

1. Kishore has *less* trust in his brother *than* on me.

2. I have *less* money in my pocket *than* you.

(ii) *Lesser,* on the other hand means not so great in size etc., than the other one, but remember that *lesser* is never followed by than.

1. Between smoking and drinking, smoking is a *lesser* evil.

2. A *lesser* man would have given some bribe to get his promotion, but not so Abdul Ghâfoor.

b. *Outermost, uttermost, utmost*

(i) *Outermost* means something farthest away.

1. An armed sentry was posted on the *outermost* point near the international border.

(ii)*uttermost* is most remote or distant.

2. From the top of the Golconda Fort, one may see the *uttermost* part of Hyderabad.

(iii) *utmost* the extreme limit, the maximum limit :

3. This is the *utmost* I can do for you. Don't expect me to give you any more help.

c. *Many, a great many, many a*

Remember that while *many* refers to number, *much* is *used* for only quantity.

1. There are *many* answers to this question.
2. There were *many* people in the shop.
3. He didn't offer me *much* help in my hour of need.

(i) *A great many* stresses a large number

1. *A great many* people had come to listen to the speaker.
2. My little brother has *a great many* toys to play with.

(ii) *Many a* is an expression that uses a singular form to suggest plural in meaning. It stresses a single person's experience to suggest that there are many others like him.

1. *Many a* man feels scared at the sight of a cobra.
2. *Many an* ignorant man pretends that he knows too much.

d. *Little, a little, the little*

(i) *Little* means almost nothing, hardly anything.

1. There is *little* possibility of his getting the job.

2. There is *little* chance of her getting married now that she is forty-four.

(ii) *A Little* means not much, but some.

1. I have *a little* hope to go abroad.
2. This team has *a little* hope to win the match.
3. '*A little* knowledge is a dangerous thing . . .'

(iii) *The Little* is an expression that refers to some quantity readily available. Since it cannot stand by itself, it must be followed by something else it refers to.

1. From *the little* I know about the man, he is not trustworthy.
2. I gave him *the little* money I had but he did not look satisfied.

e. *Few, a few, the few*

While *few* means none, hardly any, *a few* means a limited number, not many.

1. When I reached the meeting there were *few* people there. I thought I had come there too early.
2. I have *a few* suggestions for you, if you'd care to consider any of them.

The few is a phrase which means a limited number, but it must be followed by something to define its meaning.

1. *The few* books I had I gifted to a public library.
2. I was not greeted by *the few* guests I knew at the party.

f. *elder, older, oldest, eldest*

Elder is never followed by *than*, and it is used only for persons, not animals. Both *elder* and *eldest* are usually used while referring to the same family.

1. Prasad is my *elder* brother.
2. Shiela is his *elder* sister.
3. Ram Prasad is the *eldest* in the family.

Older and *oldest* are adjectives that primarily refer to the age of a person (a member of a family or anyone) or object.

1. Samuel is *older* than his sister Nancy.
2. My car is *older* than yours.
3. This dog is *older* than the other one.
4. My grandfather is the *oldest* resident in this locality.

g. *farther, further*

Farther (from far, not near) refers to distance.

1. As we went *farther* down the road, we recognized his factory.
2. He has taken a view much *farther* from reality.

Further means going beyond a certain point (not implying distance)

1. As I looked *further* into the contract, I felt that I should not sign it.
2. This matter needs some *further* discussion.
3. I advise you to wait for *further* orders from your department.

(N.B. In current usage, however, *further* is something used in place of *farther*.)

h. *Later, latest, latter, last*

(i) *Later* and *latest* are adjectives that refer to time.

1. There is a *later* train to Nagpur.
2. Is there a *later* edition of this dictionary?
3. He arrived much *later* for the interview.
4. What is the *latest* news about his health?
5. This appears to be the *latest* fashion of sun-glasses.
6. This is the *latest* model of Fiat.

(ii) *Latter* and *last* are adjectives that signify position or order. For example :

1. Of the two trains available for Delhi, the *latter* would suit my convenience.

2. Although Ram and Shyam are both very friendly, I prefer the *latter*.

3. I was the *last* to arrive for the interview.

4. This seems to be the *last* straw on the camel's back.

TASK 1

Compare yourself with others:

In the boxes below write your own name and those of two of your friends or cousins. (X and Y). Give yourself and the other two a score of 1-5 for each of the activities listed below:

0 — very poor
5 — excellent

	own name	X	Y
sing	3	2	5
dance			
write neatly			
dress smartly			
run fast			
work hard			
speak English fluently			
play cricket			

Using this information, now make at least ten sentences like the following.

Y sings **better** than me but X sings **worse** than me.

TASK 2

Each of the following items has three or four answers marked (a), (b), (c) and (d). Only one of these is correct. Choose the correct response to fill the blanks in the sentence.

1. Ramesh is ————— you.

   (a) older than (b) elder than (c) older to (d) elder to

2. This dress is ————— to that one.

   (a) preferable (b) more better (c) more preferable (d) most preferable

3. The speed of this aeroplane is ————— .

(a) higher than the other one
(b) higher than the other aeroplane
(c) higher than that of the other plane.
(d) higher

4. Out of these two novels, this is __________ .

(a) most enjoyable (b) more enjoyable (c) best (d) better enjoyable

5. My school is __________ .

(a) superior to his (b) superior than his (c) superior (d) most superior

6. My sister is __________ of the two.

(a) the tallest (b) tall (c) taller (d) the taller

7. This cyclone in Orissa was __________ than the previous one.

(a) worst (b) badder (c) worse (d) bad

8. My __________ brother is an engineer.

(a) elder (b) older (c) old

9. Our teacher came __________ than us to school yesterday.

(a) latter (b) late (c) later (d) more late

10. The first part of the movie is interesting but the __________ half is boring.

(a) second (b) latter (c) later (d) last

TASK 3

Compare and contrast modern times with the olden times.

Use as many comparative adjectives as you can to describe the people, the lifestyle, the living conditions etc.

e.g. In olden days, the people were **more relaxed** and **friendlier** than in modern times.

- -

- -

THE MAN **WHO INTRODUCED THE VIOLIN**

Relative Clauses: Restrictive and Non-restrictive

The person **who introduced the violin into Indian music** was Vadivelu. He was a musician **who lived in the Travancore court in the 1830s.** Swati Thirunal, **who was the Maharaja of Travancore,** bought three violins and gave them to Vadivelu. Vadivelu showed how well Carnatic music could be played on this strange new instrument. Vadivelu was such a master that Swati Thirunal gave him an ivory violin, **which his descendants still have in their home.**

Who introduced the violin into Indian music?

- -

Who was Vadivelu?

- -

Who was Swati Thirunal?

- -

What do the descendants of Vadivelu have in their home?

- -

Look carefully at the clauses marked in bold in the passage. These clauses help us to identify the man or musician we are talking about.

Which man? Not any man but this particular man **who introduced the violin** was Vadivelu. Who was he? Not any musician, but a musician **who lived in the Travancore courts in the 1830s.** These clauses are like adjectives. They are therefore called **adjectival clauses** or **relative clauses.** The clauses in bold here are **restrictive relative clauses** because they restrict the meaning of the noun **musician** and **man** and they cannot be omitted.

Now, look at the following sentences:

Swati Thirunal, **who was the Maharaja of Travancore**, bought three violins.

Swati Thirunal gave him an ivory violin, **which his descendants still have in their home.**

In these cases, the underlined clauses do not help in the identification of Swati Thirunal or the violin. They just provide additional information. They can be omitted and yet the sentences can be understood. These are **non-restrictive relative clauses.** A non-restrictive relative clause is always indicated by commas in writing and by a pause in speech.

TASK 1

Match the following personalities ***who have made history*** *(for better or for worse) with the correct description. Write it as a sentence using a relative clause.*

e.g. Mahatma Gandhi — Led the Indian nation to freedom and set an example for non-violent protest.

This man is Mahatma Gandhi, **who led the Indian nation to freedom.** He is the one **who set an example for non-violent protest.**

Nelson Mandela — Changed the face of modern China, with far-reaching consequence for the world.

Mahatma Gandhi — Brought an end to apartheid in Africa

Adolf Hitler — Led the Indian nation to freedom, and set an example for non-violent protest.

Mao-Tse Tung — Instrumental in the devastation caused by World War II.

Jawaharlal Nehru — Despite modern day criticism, he is still seen as the architect of modern India.

Alfred Nobel — Invented dynamite and has prizes in his name.

Mother Teresa — Symbol of British conservative national, won World War II for the allies

Winston Churchill — Symbol of courage and compassion.

TASK 2

Can you identify these sportspersons? Write a line or two describing them using (1) a restrictive relative clause and (2) a non-restrictive relative clause.

e.g. This man **who has long hair** is David Beckham.(restrictive relative clause)

David Beckham, **who is a football player**, is the favourite of many teenagers. (non-restrictive relative clause)

(Pictures of Rahul Dravid, Leander Paes, Steffi Graf, Kapil Dev, Viswanathan Anand, Anju George, Karnam Malleswari, Sachin Tendulkar, Gopichand, Ronaldo.)

1) ________________________________

____

2) ________________________________

____

3) ________________________________

____

4) ________________________________

____

5) ________________________________

____

6) ________________________________

____

7) ________________________________

____

8) ________________________________

____

9) ________________________________

----

10) ---------------------------------

TASK 3

Combine the following sentences using a relative clause.

e.g. Agra was once the capital of the Mughal empire in the 16th and early 18th century. It is one and a half hours by express train from Delhi.

Agra, which was once the capital of the Mughal empire in the 16th and early 18th century is one and a half hours by express train from Delhi.

1. Tourists come from all over the world. They make a pilgrimage to Taj Mahal.

   ----

2. The Taj Mahal is India's most famous architectural wonder. It reminds visitors about the rich civilization of our country.

   ----

3. The postcard picture of Taj Mahal does not adequately convey the legend, the poetry and the romance of the monument. Rabindranath Tagore called it 'a teardrop on the cheek of time'.

   ----

4. Taj Mahal means 'Crown Palace'. It is in fact the most well preserved and architecturally beautiful tomb in the world.

   ----

5. Taj Mahal stands on the bank of River Yamuna. It serves as a wide moat defending the Great Red Fort of Agra.

   ----

6. It was built by the fifth Mughal emperor, Shah Jahan in 1631 in memory of his second wife, Mumtaz Mahal. She was a Muslim Persian princess.

----

7. She died while accompanying her husband in Burhanpur in a campaign. The campaign was to crush a rebellion.

----

8. The Taj Mahal was built in her memory. It is a 'symbol of eternal love'.

----

9. The Taj rises on a high red sandstone base. It is topped by a huge white marble terrace on which rests the famous dome flanked by four tapering minarets.

----

10. Within the dome lies the jewel-inlaid cenotaph of the queen. It is an example of exquisite workmanship.

TASK 4

Find out the person (Refer to an encyclopedia or search on the Net if you don't know)

1. who invented a method of reading for the blind.
2. who invented the passenger lift.
3. who was a musician in Akbar's court.
4. who wrote 'Alice in Wonderland'.
5. who was the Aryan god of sea and sky.

Write a paragraph using as many relative clauses as you can.

TASK 5

Imagine you are the Director of a company. You would like to appoint a Marketing Manager. Write an advertisement using the clues given below: Use relative clauses.

WANTED

A Marketing Manager __________ is a postgraduate, __________ preferably an MBA degree __________ at least 5 years of marketing experience.

A man who is __________ dynamic, outgoing, good communication skills, willing to travel a lot.

Anyone with these qualities can apply to
The Director,
Alpha Pvt. Ltd.
P.B. 1641.
Hyderabad.

e.g. WANTED

A marketing manager **who is a postgraduate,** preferably with an MBA degree.

BABY SLEEPS

Describing Habitual Actions: The Simple Present Tense

BABY SLEEPS

The baby **wept;**
The mother **took** it from the nurse's arms,
And **hushed** its fears, and **soothed** its vain alarms,
And baby **slept.**

Again it **weeps,**
And God doth **take** it from the mother's arms,
From present griefs, and future unknown harms,
And baby **sleeps.**

What did the mother do when the baby wept?

What does God always do when the baby weeps?

The first stanza of the poem describes an incident in the past—i.e. when the baby wept and what the mother did then. On the other hand, the second stanza describes what God always does to babies when they cry. The poet has used the **simple past tense** to describe the incident in the past and the **simple present tense** to describe what is always done. i.e. habitual action.

The simple present tense is used to describe:

i. Habitual actions or actions that are repeated e.g. I (always) **take** a taxi to office.

ii. Definite future events e.g. The college **reopens** on the 20th of June.

iii. Past events (to make it sound dramatic) e.g. I saw a horror film last evening. In that film, a ghost **comes** to the girl's house every night at 12 o'clock!

iv. Instantaneous actions (as in commentaries) e.g. The President **goes** past the guard of honour and **waves** to the crowd.

TASK 1

Read the following poem:

Macavity's a ginger cat; he's very tall and thin;
You would know him if you saw him, for his eyes **are** sunken in,
His brow **is** deeply lined with thought; his head **is** highly domed;
His coat **is** dusty with neglect, his whiskers **are** uncombed.
He **sways** his head from side to side, with movements like a snake;
And when you **think** he's half asleep, he's always wide-awake.

Who is Macavity?

Describe Macavity.

What does he do usually?

TASK 2

Unusual professions

Do you know who a gerontologist is?

Gerontology is the study of the elderly, and of the aging process itself. So, a gerontologist **studies** elderly people and their problems.

The term comes from Geriatrics, which is the study of the diseases of the elderly.

Can you write a short paragraph on the following unusual professions? Use the simple present tense to describe what these people do always. Refer to a good dictionary to find out the meanings of words you do not know.

1. an archaeologist
2. an exchequer
3. a game keeper
4. a phrenologist
5. a solicitor

TASK 3

Use the correct form of the verb given in brackets.

All mammals ————(have) the same basic eye construction, but it ————(be) the position of the eyes on the head that ————(determine) what or how much an animal ————(see). Predators, such as cats, ————(need) to focus their vision exactly to pinpoint their prey. Their eyes, therefore, ————(focus) together on an object. This ————(enable) them to judge where an object or prey is in relation to everything in front of them. Mammals that ————(live) in open country, such as the plains of Africa, ————(follow) the rule of having their eyes situated on their head according to whether they ————(hunter or hunted).

TASK 4

Read the following poem by Harindranath Chattopadhyay titled 'The Rainbow'.

'Look at the rainbow up the sky there right overhead
V, I, B, G and Y, O and R:
These are the seven colours that glow in the rainbow ring…
Do you not think that the rainbow is ever a beautiful thing?

There was a time when I used to think that the rainbow was
A wonderful God in his Heaven paints and draws,
Or garland of seven colours by the sweet angels hung:
That was the way I was taught by my mother when I was young .

> But today I know very well that the rainbow is not that,
> It is neither a circle painted by God nor a garland of glows
> Hung by the angels aloft, as I once was led to suppose.
>
> It is just an event that occurs when the ray of light pass through
> Small points of dust and globules of water hanging like dew
> In the high-speed air-and the white light breaks hues which melt
> One into the other, forming the rainbow's magical belt . . .'

The poet says in the poem that
'There was a time when I **used to** think that the rainbow was
A wonderful God in His heaven paints and draws . . .'
'Used to' refers to a habit or a state that existed in the past but which has not continued up till now.

Write a short paragraph (50–75 words using the clues given below) describing how people in India **used to** lead their life in the olden days.

Lead a calm and peaceful life—no television, computers or other modern gadgets-- live in joint family—wake up early—go to the fields for cultivation—have an elaborate meal—return home early—spend time with the family members—go to bed early as the sun sets.

Begin as:

In the olden days, the people of India **used to** lead a calm and peaceful life...

Contrast this to how they we lead our life today.

I HAVE BEEN EATING

Temporary Actions in Progress: Present Perfect Continuous Tense

Renota Arganza spent several days at sea clinging to a buoy after his boat capsized off the Philippines. When he was rescued, the people around him asked. 'How did you survive?' He answered, 'I have been eating my underpants piece by piece.'

Renota wants to tell them that from the time his boat capsized till the time he was rescued, he had been eating his underpants. He wants to emphasize on the temporariness (hopefully?) and continuity of this action!

The present perfect continuous tense relates an action which began in the past and which continues up to the present moment. It emphasizes the **temporariness** of this action.

	Singular	Plural
1st person	I have been eating	we have been eating
2nd person	You have been eating	You have been eating
3rd person	He has been eating She has been eating It has been eating	They have been eating

TASK 1

The following people all have certain temporary habits.

From the clues given below, frame sentences to describe their habits.

a woman collecting stamps	a boy learning tabla	a man smoking
a girl playing badminton	a woman writing poems	a baby biting her mother

e.g. Mrs. Lalitha/collect stamps/ 10 years.

Mrs. Lalitha **has been collecting stamps** for the last ten years.

1) Rohit / learn tabla / six months.

2) Mr. Prasad / smoke cigarettes / three years.

3) Lalitha / play badminton / one week.

4) Mrs. Murthy / write poems / five years

5) My daughter / bite me / two days.

TASK 2

Read and answer the questions.

The Slow Food movement founded by an Italian more than a decade ago **has been doing** well in the USA where its membership **has been growing.**

The promoters of this movement **have been opposing** fast food and hasty eating habits and **have been encouraging** people to have long leisurely dinners with their families. The emblem of this movement is a snail.

1. What has been doing well in the USA?
2. What have the promoters of this movement been opposing?
3. What have they been encouraging people to do?
4. Is it a popular movement? How do you know?
5. Have you been eating too much of fast food?

TASK 3

Joy of Brotherhood

Fill in the blanks using either the ***Present Perfect*** *or the* ***Present Perfect Continuous form*** *of the verbs given in brackets.*

'Daddy, can you get me another ball?' It was my brother Krishna a chubby, ten-year-old.

'You ____________ (lose) balls. This is the fifth ball ____________

(lose). You ____________ (be) very careless,' my father shouted. He added, 'I ____________ (have) enough of this. I'm not going to get you a new ball this time.'

At night when I went to bed, my brother said:

'I ____________ (pray) all this while to God to give me a ball. I wish that all the balls belonging to the children in the neighbourhood would fall into our backyard. If not all, at least one.'

I felt like laughing. The next morning, my brother ran up to me and said:

'Look ! I ____________ (find) one ! God ____________ (answer) my prayers. I found this is in our backyard.'

'You ____________ always ____________ (keep) your things very carefully. So please keep my ball too safely.' Saying this, Krishna handed the ball over to me. It was my brother's own lost ball! But I did not tell him that. To this day, my brother ____________ not (sleep) a night without thanking God!

TASK 4

Describe five of your present hobbies in a paragraph.

Eg: **I have been collecting** WWF cards. I **have been collecting** these cards because I am interested in wrestling. I **have been watching** all the wrestling matches on the television. Hulk Hogan is my favourite wrestler. He **has been competing** in all the major events . . .

- -

- -

- -

- -

THE BOTTLE HAD TRAVELLED **A LONG DISTANCE**

The Past Tense versus the Past Perfect Tense

An eight-year-old boy put a message in a plastic bottle and threw it in the sea hoping it would be found—and it was eventually picked up six months later!

However, the bottle <u>had travelled</u> around 15000 miles from Britain to Australia, before it was discovered.

James Burch in Britain wrote a joke with his address on some paper and threw it out to sea in a bottle, while on a day trip to the seaside.

Six months later the bottle was found floating in the Indian Ocean by Charles Cross, a chemistry researcher, in Perth, Australia. Charles wrote back to James and included the boy's note as proof of finding the bottle.

James's brother David also threw a bottle into the sea at the same time but, as yet, he hasn't received a reply.

The boys' dad Terry said: 'I didn't expect either of the bottles to be seen again.'

Imagine that the boy threw the bottle into the sea in December 1998. This bottle was found after six months later i.e. in June 1999 in Australia.

December 1998	June 1999	Now 2004
bottle thrown into the sea	bottle found	

↓

The bottle **had travelled** for six months. It **had travelled** 15,000 miles from Britain to Australia.

We use the simple past tense to talk about the past i.e. After six months, in June 1999 a researcher **found** the bottle.

To talk about past in past i.e. to refer to what had happened before the past event (i.e. discovery of the bottle in June 1999) we use the past perfect tense.

The boy **had thrown** the bottle into the sea in December 1998.

When the bottle was found, it **had travelled** for six months.

When we use the past perfect tense, we are comparing two events in the past, one happening before the other. The past perfect gives us a way to show which event happened first and which one followed.

i. I **could not enter** my house. I **had forgotten** my key.

ii. The teacher **had already left** when the student **arrived.**

- When comparing two events, if 'before' or 'after' is used, the simple past can be used instead because the relationship of time is already clear.

After the students left, the entire staff **had** a meeting.

Past perfect tense

Subject		Verb
I		travelled
We	had	believed
You		found
He		
She		
It		
They		

- Unnecessary use of past perfect tense

Incorrect: The teacher **had explained** the lesson last week. ×
Correct: The teacher **explained** the lesson last week. ✓

Simple sentences with one verb occurring in the past most often require only simple past tense. Past perfect tense is necessary only when two verbs occur in the past, one before the other.

TASK 1

The following was the list of holiday homework given by Aditya's teachers. When college reopened, Aditya ***had done*** *only some of it. Look at the table below to see what he had done and what he* ***hadn't done****. Make sentences like:*

When the college reopened, Aditya **had written** his **English essay but he hadn't drawn the map in Geography.**

Holiday Homework	Task done	Task not done
	✓	×
Write an essay in English on 'Pollution'.	✓	
Solve the equations in Chemistry.		×
Solve the problems on pg.103 in the math book.	✓	
Draw and label the respiratory system of man.	✓	
Explain the proverbs on pg.85 in the Hindi textbook.		×
Prepare the charts in your practical notebook.		×

TASK 2

Change the verbs given in brackets into either the simple past or the past perfect tense (according to the meaning).

e.g. We (be) prepared for the English test because our teacher (inform) us about it.

We **were** prepared for the English test because our teacher **had informed** us about it.

1. Ashok (reach) the station at 10 a.m. The train (leave) at 9.30 a.m. So Ashok (miss) the train.
2. When I (go) home, I (find) that my father already (reach) home before me.
3. Last year, Mr. Rao (win) a big prize in a lottery. Until then he (be) rather poor.
4. Geeta (leave) the office late. She (work) overtime.
5. I (can) not enter my room until the sweeper (sweep) my room.
6. The school (be) very quiet after the children (leave).
7. I (return) the book in the library after I (read) it.
8. Meera (be) shocked. Her house (rob).
9. Kavita (come) home unhappy. She (miss) her flight to Calcutta.
10. The teacher (give) Arun full marks in the test. Arun (have) prepared very well for the test.

TASK 3

Read and enjoy this joke.

Mr. Anand : Poor Mr. Williams. His wife <u>left</u> him a millionaire.

Mr. Verma : Why do you feel sorry for him?

Mr. Anand : He <u>had been</u> a multimillionaire earlier.

Read and answer the following questions.

When Henri d'Orleans died in June 1999, his nine children expected to get a lot of money.

After all, their father was once ranked among France's wealthiest citizens. But to their shock and dismay they found that their father—with whom they had never got along—**had spent** all his fortune and **had left** them only half a dozen embroidered handkerchiefs and a pair of bedroom slippers.

1. What did the children expect when their father died?

----

2. Why did they expect to get a lot of money?

----

3. What had their father done?

----

4. What had their father left behind?

----

5. Were they happy?

TASK 4.

Write a newspaper report based on the outline given below. Use the simple past and the past perfect tense wherever required.

Mr. and Mrs. Prakash (admit) in a hospital. They (go) for a late night movie. They (eat) at a hotel after which Mr. Prakash (drive) the car very fast. A lorry coming equally fast from the opposite direction (hit) them.

Mr. Prakash (fall) unconscious immediately. Mrs. Prakash (be) badly injured.

A crowd (gather) around the car. They ———— immediately (inform) the police and (call) for an ambulance.

It (be) a nightmare for Mr. and Mrs. Prakash

Mumbai, 2 October 2001

....

....

....

....

....

....

TASK 5

Fill in the blanks with the simple past or the past perfect form of the verb given in brackets.

Rahul ————(go) to his village after twenty years. Everything ———— ————(change). The tall red building was the school where he ————(study) up to class X. Rahul ————(peep) into the classroom. This was where he ———— ——(play) tricks on his friends!

Rahul ————(walk) to the city center. With great difficulty, Rahul ————(find) his favourite sweet shop. As a child, he ————(eat) the best sweets in this shop. Rahul ————(long) for those sweets again.

Rahul finally ————(reach) the old two storied house in Nehru Nagar. This was the house where he ————(spend) fifteen years of his life. Rahul ———— (examine) every nook and corner of the house carefully. How he ————(wish) he ————(not leave) the village and gone to the city!

IT **CAN'T** BE A VASE, IT **MUST** BE TWO FACES

Indicating Probability, Possibility and Certainty: use of 'can', 'could', 'may', 'might' and 'must'

Dhiru and Veeru were looking at a picture and quarrelling. 'It is a vase,' said Dhiru.

'Of course not. It can't be. It is two people facing each other,' argued Veeru. 'Can't you see the top and bottom and the V-shape? It must be a vase,' continued Dhiru.

'Can't you see the nose and mouth of the two people?' exclaimed Veeru.

Mr. Shekhar, their father was curious to see the picture.

'Show me the picture,' he said.

This was the picture that had caused the quarrel between the two brothers.

'Both of you are right. It **could** be a vase or two people.'

He explained, 'Dhiru, you **must** have looked at the black part; so it is a vase for you. Veeru you must have looked at the white portion; so it is two persons for you.'

Dhiru was certain that it was a vase and Veeru was certain that it was two people facing each other.

To express possibility, probability and certainty, we use

can, could, may, might and must.

impossible——>	improbable——>	probable——>	possible
can't	couldn't	could	may
	mightn't	might	can

If we are certain about something, we use 'can't'. However, if we are unsure, we use 'couldn't' or 'mightn't'.

e.g. Suppose you are woken up in the middle of the night by some sounds in the kitchen. You wonder who it is. So you would say: It can't be a ghost (because you know there are no ghosts!).

You might say: It couldn't be a thief (but you are unsure because a thief might have broken the latch and entered the house).

TASK 1

Imagine you are a doctor.
A patient comes to you with high fever and vomiting.
You look at his symptoms and try to diagnose his illness.
You discuss with other doctors the different possibilities and finally conclude that he has malaria.

Write the dialogue between you and the other doctors.

e.g. You : He has high fever. **Could** it be a viral infection?

Doctor A: It **could** also be typhoid.

Doctor B: I think it **might be** . . .

Continue using the clues given below :

body – yellow – jaundice ------------------------------------

lung infection – pneumonia ------------------------------------

High fever – shivering – malaria ------------------------------------

TASK 2

The Lair

There was a time when snakes could talk. The snake that lived in the Garden of Eden had one habit that Eve was not aware of. The snake told the truth only on four days of the week. He was untruthful on Tuesday, Thursday and Saturdays.
One day he said to Eve: 'Eve, Why don't you eat an apple?'
'I'm not allowed to', said Eve.
'You **can** eat it today,' said the snake. 'Today is Saturday and God is resting.'
'I'll eat it tomorrow,' said Eve.
'Tomorrow is Wednesday and it will be too late,' said the reptile.
Eve did not know the days of the week so she ate the apple.
What could/ couldn't be the day of the week when this conversation took place? Use 'could' or 'might' to indicate possibilities.

Answer :

It **could** only have taken place on one of the days that the snake was given to lying. It **could** not have taken place on Saturday because then the snake would have told the truth, at least, partly. It **could** not have been Tuesday, for the same reason. So the conversation **must** have taken place on a Thursday.

TASK 3

Prepare a chart on pollution stating different possibilities for pollution in cities.

e.g. Pollution in cities **could** be due to the increase in the number of vehicles on the road.

TASK 4

Read the following newspaper report.

TRAIN DERAILS
123 KILLED
MANY INJURED

The Andhra Pradesh Express coming from New Delhi derailed about 100 km. from Ballarshah last night. 123 passengers were killed and many were injured. The Railway Minister has ordered an enquiry into this matter.

The Railway Minister questions the General Manager of Railways about the various possible reasons for this derailment.

1. Discuss in pairs what the Minister and the General Manager must/could have said to each other.

2. Write a dialogue between the Minister and the General Manager.
   e.g. The General Manager: Sir, the driver **could** have been careless.

Railway Minister : ____

____

General Manager : ____

____

TASK 5

This is a painting done by Ramesh.

Prabhu and Prakash are fighting over what this could be:

What could it be?

Think of five possibilities. Use could or might to suggest the possibilities or **must** if you are certain as to what it is.

Is this man playing a sax, or is there something more here?

____

____

____

____

____

BE BOWLED OVER!

Active and Passive

Here is an interesting incident in cricket to bowl you over[1] !

It was a test series match between India and England. Madan Lal was playing the first test in England. He <u>**was clean bowled**</u> by Mike Hendricks for 2. The off and leg stump <u>**were knocked out**</u> of the ground, but the middle stump was standing!

Here is another interesting report.

A strange dismissal **was reported** from Kalgoorlie in South Australia. The batsman, Stan Dawson, **was hit** on the thigh by a fast delivery. He had a box of matches in his pocket. This **was ignited**. He was **run out** as he tried to put out the flames!

Look at the following sentences:

Madan Lal **was clean bowled** by Mike . . . The off and leg stump **were knocked** out . . . Stan Dawson **was hit** on the thigh . . . The box of matches **was ignited**..

In these sentences, the emphasis is on what was done rather than on who did them.

1. To bowl over: to surprise you. E.g. I was bowled over by the beautiful scenery.

These are **passive** constructions.

e.g. Mike **clean bowled** Madan Lal.(Active)
Madan Lal **was clean bowled** by Mike.(Passive)

Mike **knocked down** the stumps. (Active)
The stumps **were knocked down** (by Mike). (Passive)

The subject of a sentence is the word/ phrase/clause that tells us who is doing something or what/who something is.

e.g. The boys are playing cricket.
They are extremely noisy while playing cricket.

The object of a sentence is the word/phrase/clause that is affected or on which something is done.

e.g. The boys are throwing the ball.
Oh my God! The ball has broken the window pane.

In a passive sentence, the subject and the object change their positions.

Note the changes given below.

i. The direct object becomes the subject. e.g. Madan Lal (object)———> (subject)

ii. The verb is changed to the 'be+ past participle form'. e.g. clean bowled——>was clean bowled

iii. The subject is either deleted or moved to the object of a preposition. e.g. (by Mike)

ACTIVE	PASSIVE
The mother loves her baby dearly.	The baby is loved by his mother dearly.
The baby ate rice for lunch.	Rice was eaten by the baby for lunch.
The mother is carrying the baby.	The baby is being carried by its mother.
The mother has carried the baby for an hour.	The baby has been carried by its mother for an hour.
The mother will take the baby home.	The baby will be taken home by his mother.
The mother ought to leave the baby at home now.	The baby ought to be left at home by the mother now.

Stay active!

There are certain do's and don'ts with regard to the use of passives.

- A passive construction is used only when the doer of an action is unknown or unimportant or when the receiver is to be focused.

e.g.
My son hit my daughter.
-becomes-
My daughter was hit by my son.
-or-
My daughter was hit.

Consider the above sentences. The second choice (My daughter was hit by my son.) actually emphasizes the brother's role. Whereas 'My daughter was hit' hides the fact that it was my son who hit her.

Thus, the passive can be used to hide an agent (when it's deleted) or to emphasize one (when it's expressed).

e.g. My neighbour was murdered last evening. (Who murdered him is here unknown)
English is taught at this Institute. (Who teaches it is here unimportant)
Sachin Tendulkar was chosen as the best player of the year. (The receiver i.e. Sachin Tendulkar is focused).

- **Be direct in your approach. Use the active construction wherever possible.**

e.g. 'I'd be glad if you could receive me at the airport tomorrow.' ✓
is much better than saying
'I'd be glad if I could be received by you tomorrow at the airport.' ✗
We are undertaken all party orders. ✗
We undertake all party orders. ✓

It is not possible to construct passives of verbs like 'die', 'sleep', 'run', jump', 'cost', weigh', 'resemble' 'happen'

e.g. The race was run by the athletes from Nepal. ✗
He is resembled by his uncle. ✗
It was happened by chance. ✗

- **With verbs like 'need' 'ought to' and 'has to' the passive form has to be used.**

e.g The copier needs fixed. ✗
The form ought to completed. ✗
The copier needs to be fixed. ✓
The form ought to be completed. ✓

TASK 1

Given below is a flow chart on how salt is made.

Write a paragraph describing how salt is made. Use the sentences given in the flow chart in the passive form.

e.g. The salt veins in the deep mines **are broken** by explosives.

Break salt veins in deep mines by explosives	Send it to various users
↓	↑
Carry this salt to the surface on elevators	Pack the salt
↓	↑
Put the salt in a crusher	Sort in out
↓	↑
Separate the salt in a screen →	Take the salt to mills

TASK 2

Read the following passage and answer the questions given below.

THE JALLIANWALA BAGH TRAGEDY

On 13 April 1919, at 4.30 p.m., a large crowd gathered at the Jallianwala Bagh in Amritsar. They were unaware that a ban on public meetings **had been imposed** by General Dyer a couple of days before.

An angry Dyer marched into the Bagh with fifty Gurkha riflemen. Without giving any warning he ordered the troops to open fire. Three hundred and seventy-nine people **were killed** and a thousand were injured. A strict curfew was imposed in the city thereafter. No one **was allowed** to leave their homes, not even to collect the bodies of their dead. To add to their misery, both electricity and water supplies **were cut**. The incident shocked most Indians and made them fight against the British rule.

1. What was the crowd unaware of? Who had imposed this?

----

2. How many people were killed?

----

3. What was imposed after the killing?

----

4. What was not allowed during the curfew?

----

5. What was cut?

IT WAS BELIEVED THAT - - - - -:

THE USE OF IMPERSONAL PASSIVES.

Read the following interesting finding:

The set of three monkeys, one covering its eyes, another its ears and the third its mouth **is said** to **have been invented** by a Japanese priest named Dengyo in the ninth century.
He used monkeys to convey his message of the Three Don'ts because in Japanese the word for don't 'Zaru' also means monkey.
The three monkeys are:
Mi- Zaru- Don't see evil monkey
Iwa- Zaru- Don't talk evil monkey
Kika –Zaru- Don't hear evil monkey

In a newspaper report, the event is more important than the person who performed it. Hence, the passive construction is often used to make it formal and impersonal.

e.g. It **was reported** yesterday that the US bombed Iraq. It **is believed** that thousands were killed.

TASK 3

Expand the following newspaper headlines. Use the passive form. You might have to add articles if necessary.

SHAH RUKH KHAN GIVEN BEST ACTOR AWARD

Shah Rukh Khan was given the best actor award.

1. 260 PASSENGERS KILLED IN TRAIN ACCIDENT.

----

2. MURDERER OF FINANCE MINISTER ARRESTED YESTERDAY.

----

3. RAID CARRIED OUT BY CBI IN DIRECTOR'S HOUSE.

----

4. PRINCE WILLIAMS SENT TO BOARDING SCHOOL.

----

5. DOG BITTEN IN ANGER BY MAN.

TASK 4

Rewrite each of the following sentences in the active voice:

1. The students in the hostel are being taken care of by the warden.

----

2. The results of the students have been withheld by the office.

----

3. Admission to any course cannot be given by the Institute automatically.

----

4. A complete change of the office set up was brought about by the Director..

----

5. The student was asked by the teacher why he had lied.

----

6. The difficult question was answered by Harish, who was the brightest boy in class.

----

7. The most important thing, i.e. the printing of invitation cards is being done by the father of the bridegroom.

----

8. The proposal has to be approved by an expert committee before it is implemented.

----

9. The passive construction is most often used by Indians instead of the active.

----

10. The passive voice must be avoided by writers if they want to make their writing direct and interesting.

TASK 5

Rewrite the following sentences as impersonal passives:

1. Reporters reported on the earthquake in Delhi.

e.g. It **was reported** that there was an earthquake in Delhi yesterday.

2. People believe that it caused severe damage.

----

3. People say that it was unexpected.

----

4. People think that the earthquake is due to global warming.

----

5. Reporters reported that there might be another earthquake soon in Central India.

TASK 6

Read the following report.

They Eat Meat Too

It **was believed** that chimpanzees were vegetarian until the American scientist Jane Goodall showed that this was not true. Chimpanzees **were studied** for several years in the Gombe National park in Tanzania by Ms Goodall, where it **was discovered** that though they were largely vegetarian, they also hunted down prey for meat.

Invent a story on any of the following topics and present it as a news item.

e.g. Here is the news. It is **believed / reported / thought / felt / said** - - - - -

1. The reappearance of a dinosaur.

2. The invention of a grammar cap by Mr.Martin that can solve all problems in grammar.

The miraculous rescue of passengers on Boeing 747 flight to Mumbai.

SILKY **TURNS UP** AFTER NINE MONTHS

Creating and Extending Meanings: Phrasal and Prepositional Verbs

Read the following

There are many stories of cats trekking hundreds of miles to return to a place they regard as home.

Silky was one such cat. His Australian owners took him on a caravan holiday to a place near Brisbane where he promptly got lost. He did not **turn up** till the end of the vacation. His owners felt that he was probably **run over** by a vehicle somewhere and so returned to their home in Melbourne, more than 2,320 km away, without him. But their fears **turned out** to be wrong ! Nine months later, Silky appeared on their doorstep, weak and **run out** of his vibrant energy.

A number of verbs in English can be used with an adverb or a preposition to mean something completely new.

e.g. turn up, turn into

run over, run out

These combinations are called **phrasal verbs.**

Look at the list of phrasal verbs that can be formed with **turn** :

i. turn up = arrive, appear
ii. turn into = become

iii. turn down = refuse
iv. turn on = attack
v. turn out = happen in the end
vi. turn on = switch on
vii. turn off = switch off
viii. turn (somebody) away = send them from the door

The following are some of the phrasal verbs which can be formed with **run** :

i. run over = rushed / killed by a vehicle
ii. run out (of) = exhausted, have no more
iii. run away with = steal and carry off
iv. run through = look at quickly / repeat.

TASK 1

A. *Replace the underlined verbs in the sentences below with a phrasal verb beginning with* ***turn***.

1. By the time we went for the function, the Chief Guest had already **arrived.**

2. **Switch off** the light after you leave the room.

3. Please come home for dinner. I hope you won't **refuse** my invitation.
By pulling it in front, this sofa can **become** a bed.

4. I did not want to be disturbed, so I **asked** the salesman **to leave.**

B. *Replace the underlined verbs in the sentences below with a phrasal verb beginning with* ***run***.

1. The car has stopped because we **have no more** of petrol.

2. The police recovered the body of the young man. He was (killed) **crushed** by an express train.

3. I'm playing the role of Cleopatra in the school play. I have to **repeat** the dialogue many times to remember them.

4. When I got off my car to buy some vegetables some boys **stole** my purse.

5. I have to withdraw some money from the bank because I **have no more** money.

TASK 2

Use any one of the following phrasal verbs in the blanks given below:

run away	turn out	turn into	run through	turn away
turn down	run into	run out	turn off	turn up

When I went to Delhi, I ___________ my old school friend, Shanti. We were excited and ___________ the adventures we had in our childhood.

'Do you remember, Shanti?' I asked, 'You once asked your mother for a new dress but she ___________ it ___________. So you got angry and ___________ from home. You spent the entire day at my place. Your parents got worried as you did not ___________ home at the usual time in the evening.'

'And do you remember, Prema?' Shanti continued. 'You did not want to meet Sheela when she came home at night, you made me ___________ the lights and I tried to ___________ her ___________ at the door itself. Finally, it ___________ that she wanted to meet me and not you!'

'Shanti, you are the same,' I exclaimed, 'I thought you would ___________ a snob and not talk to me. But you are the same giggling girl.'

Finally, we ___________ of our childhood stories and went together to Hotel Paradise for lunch.

TASK 3

Read and enjoy this joke.

Magician : Look at this ball. Now I'll **turn** it **into** a rabbit.

Johnny : That isn't great. I can go down the road and **turn into** a lane !

TASK 4

Write a paragraph using the clues given below.

One day ___ my sister ___ not **turn up** from school ___ worried ___ inform police ___ sent search party ___ became 10 o'clock in the night ___ **turn into** a nightmare ___ finally **turn out** she had gone for a movie with a friend. Even though my sister **turn down** the offer ___ friend forced her ___ sister scolded for not informing us her whereabouts.

LOOKING FOR DIAMONDS

Prepositional Verbs

Frenchman August Rabot went to the Amazon to **look for** diamonds. He didn't **succeed in** finding any—instead, he fell dangerously ill and was **looked after** by the tribals in that village.

One day, while he was resting beside a stream near the village, he saw small beautifully coloured fish darting about in the clear waters of the stream. He was fascinated by the fish. He **thought of** taking these fish to Europe. Giving up his **search for** diamonds, he returned to Paris with the fish instead. As he had expected, everyone showed interest in this fish. He **explained to** everyone the origin of this fish. He began to breed and sell the fish and made a fortune in the process.

(Today the fish are seen in aquariums around the world. They are called NEON TETRAS.)

There are some verbs in English which are followed by a preposition. They are called prepositional verbs. A prepositional verb is a two part verb.

e.g.: look for (something or somebody)
succeed in
look after (somebody)
think of (something)
search for (someone or something)
explain something to (somebody)

TASK 1

For each of the following sentences, there are four answers. Select the correct one and fill in the blank.

e.g. When I am sad, I like to listen ________ some soft classical music.

(a) at (b) to (c) in (d) for
Ans : (b) to

1. I rang up my friend yesterday and congratulated him ________ getting an award.
(a) with (b) in (c) on (d) for

2. My teacher asks all the students to participate ________ the discussion.
(a) in (b) on (c) with (d) about

3. Ramesh insisted ________ going abroad after his engineering
(a) in (b) on (c) at (d) for

4. After much hard work, I succeeded ________ getting the first rank.
(a) at (b) on (c) in (d) for

5. One should not get ________ a moving bus.
(a) out (b) off (c) of (d) out of

6. For many years, my uncle has been suffering _____ cancer
(a) of (b) with (c) from (d) on

7. Shekhar always dreams ________ becoming a world famous cricketer
(a) at (b) of (c) about (d) on

8. My cousin looks exactly like my uncle. She takes ________ him
(a) for (b) of (c) after (d) from

9. One should always believe ________ God and do one's work
(a) on (b) at (c) in (d) about

10. We should prevent children ________ playing dangerous games
(a) in (b) on (c) with (d) from

TASK 2

You are the Manager of a TV manufacturing company. You want to appoint a salesman for the marketing of your TV. Write an advertisement using the clues given below: **Looking for** young, energetic salesman age 20-30-one who **believes in** talking and convincing customers. Selection will **depend on** performance at interview. Those interested, **apply for** the post within 10 days. **Wait for** a week later for the interview call.

WANTED

TASK 3

Write a letter to your friend describing your dream. Use the clues given below:

Dream of meeting Michael Jackson — one day — go to airport — to receive friend — see Michael Jackson **get off** the plane — **smile at** him — **ask for** autograph — **talk to** him — **succeed in** getting a ticket for his concert — later **write to** him — **search for** a pen fall off the bed — my mother **laugh at** me — **explain** my dream **to** her.

TASK 4

Make a survey

(a) of the kind of music your friends **listen to**
(b) who they often **dream of** meeting
(c) what courses they would like to **apply for** after their examinations

REACTING **IMMEDIATELY**

The Use of Adverbs

Presence of Mind

One day to test Birbal's bravery, Emperor Akbar **deliberately** had a mad elephant let loose in the lane through which Birbal **normally** came to Red Fort. The emperor stood in the balcony to see everything **clearly.**

Birbal was not aware of the elephant moving in that lane. **Scarcely** had he entered the lane when he saw the mad elephant coming **angrily** at him. Birbal had no weapons to defend himself. He saw a dog moving about in the lane. He reacted **immediately** and lifted the dog and threw it at the elephant **forcefully.** The dog began to cry **loudly** at the impact. He even began to scratch the elephant's forehead with his paws. The elephant was taken aback. He moved back **quickly**. Birbal came out of the lane **safely**. The emperor praised Birbal's presence of mind and gave him many gifts.

Look at these words:

deliberately	immediately
normally	forcefully
clearly	loudly
scarcely	quickly
angrily	safely

These are adverbs which are assistants to verbs. Adverbs provide some useful or necessary detail.

For example, read the following two notices. Which one is more effective for the purchase of a car? Why?

Notice 1

Wanted: An Ambassador car, which runs **smoothly** and **noiselessly**, gives **more** mileage for **less** petrol — which has been used **sparingly**.

Notice 2

Wanted: An Ambassador car, which runs, gives mileage for petrol, which has been used.

Notice 2 would be of little use in getting a car. Why? Because there must be many Ambassador cars which run and have been used. On the other hand, Notice I gives finer details which are important.

TASK 1

Make a list of the adverbs in the following passage, and opposite them put the verbs which they help to describe.

e.g. A deer was frisking along merrily

Adverb	***Verb***
merrily	*frisking*

Look up a dictionary if you do not know the meaning of a word.

The phone rang incessantly. Preeti picked it up and spoke calmly as though nothing had happened. The man with the big moustache grabbed the phone angrily from her and hung up.

'You can't play a game with me', he announced threateningly. He pushed Preeti forcefully into a dark room and locked the room firmly. Preeti looked around the room nervously. Suddenly, she spotted a ventilator at one corner. She tried desperately to reach it but couldn't. She cried miserably . . .

Now continue the story using appropriate adverbs after the verbs. You could use the clues given below:
prayed—heard noises in neighbouring room—listened—a phone mumber mentioned—remembers her mobile phone in bag—calls police—police catch he man—Preeti rescued.

TASK 2

Look at this sentence:

The milk man **tears rapidly** round the corner on his cycle everyday.
Do you know the meaning of the verb 'tears'?

Tear : go at great speed
e.g. The children **tore** out of the school gates.

Is the adverb 'rapidly' necessary to describe the verb 'tear'? No. It repeats the same information. So the adverb is unnecessary and redundant.

Look at this sentence:

My brother **whispered loudly** a secret to his friend.

Does the adverb **loudly** help in describing the verb **whisper** or does it mean the opposite?

'Whispering' means speaking softly and not loudly! So the adverb here is incorrect and unnecessary.

Are the adverbs in the following sentences unnecessary or used incorrectly? If so, rewrite the sentences.

1. The waves splashed quietly on the seashore.
2. The girl tripped slowly down the garden.
3. The audience roared loudly when the comedian joked.
4. At the party, my friends chatted conversationally.
5. Shilpa was a lazy girl who would leave her things strewn about and often her mother had to constantly pick them up after her.
6. At the scene of the accident, lot of people rushed lazily to help the injured man.
7. When there was a strong breeze, all of us shivered slowly in the bus.
8. I glanced briefly at the clock to see the time.
9. The elephant lumbered heavily and clumsily down the road.
10. When Arvind did not want to be caught by his parents for coming home late, he tiptoed noisily past their bedroom.

TASK 4

Read the following and answer the questions given below.

A teacher in a school in Beijing, China flung a book **angrily** at a fifteen-year-old student named Zhang. Zhang didn't sit **quietly**. He rushed at the teacher and bit off one of his ears **forcefully**! The ear and its owner had to be rushed to a hospital **immediately** where surgeons managed to sew the ear back **tightly** in its place!

1. How did the teacher fling the book at Zhang?

2. Did Zhang sit quietly in his place?

3. How did Zhang bite his teacher's ears?

4. What did the students do?

5. How did the surgeon sew the ear back in its place?

TASK 5

Make up sentences with a suitable adverb to describe the following.

e.g. A German (trying to) speak English — **haltingly,** or **brokenly.**

1. a young proud lady looking at the fashionable dresses in a shop

   ----

2. a young girl learning to ride a bicycle.

   ----

3. a policeman trying to control the heavy traffic.

   ----

4. a frightened old lady crossing the street in traffic.

   ----

5. an accused walking into the court room.

- **General rules regarding the use of adverbs**

1. The following are adverbs of time: **Seldom, never, ever, generally, merely, ever, often.** They are put before the verb.

e.g. He **seldom** speaks to me.

i. My mother **never** gets angry.

ii. Have you **ever** seen a blue rose?

iii.I **generally** do my homework at 6 o'clock in the evening.

iv.I **often** get up late in the morning.

2. **Much** is used with the comparative degree.

i. This book is **much** better than that one.

ii. Science is **much** easier than History.

3. **Hardly** and **scarcely** require inversion.

i. **Hardly had he gone out,** when the phone rang.

ii. **Scarcely had the students entered the class,** when the bell rang.

Select the correct answer from the four choices given below and fill in the blanks.

1. My cousin asked me ______________

(a) sing soft (b) to sing soft (c) sing softly (d) to sing softly

2. This flower ______________

(a) smells sweetly (b) smell sweetly (c) smells sweet (d) smell sweet

3. Hardly ______________, when it started raining.

(a) I went out (b) had I gone out (c) I had gone out (c) went out I

4. My sister wants to get a good grade in her final examination. So she is working ______________

(a) hardly (b) harder (c) hardest (d) hard

5. In the 1970's and 80's the situation in Punjab was tense. Nowadays, it is ______________

(a) very best (b) very better (c) much better (d) more better

6. I __________________listen to classical music.

(a) ever (b) often (c) more often (d) hard

THE MONTH OF MAY

Indicating Time: Prepositions of Time

- May Day is a festival celebrated in Europe **on** the 1st of May.
- Children's Day and Boy's Day in Japan is **on** the 5th of May.
- The Second World War ended in Europe **on** 8th of May 1945.
- According to British superstition, kittens born **in** May are not good at catching rats!

The words on and in the sentences given above tell us about the time of some event or action.

If we say:

'I woke up at six in the morning', 'at' and 'in' tell us about when the action of waking up was done.

The words on, in and at are prepositions of time as they tell us about the time of an action.

At is used to refer to an exact time

E.g. I met my friend at 8 o'clock.

On is used for particular days or months.

E.g. I joined school on 10th June.

In is used for longer periods—weeks, months, year.

E.g. I was born in July.

TASK 1

Important Events

Match the following important events with the time of their occurrence

	Event		Time
(i)	Julius Caesar was assassinated	(a)	on 9th December in 1981.
(ii)	The 'Titanic' ship sank	(b)	on 21st July in 1969
(iii)	The famous pop star John Lennon was killed	(c)	on 15th March in the year 44 BC
(iv)	Apollo 11 landed on the moon	(d)	in 1912
(v)	Thousands of people died at Jalianwalla Bagh in Amritsar	(e)	at 4.30 p.m. on April 13, 1919 1919

TASK 2

Find out when the following are celebrated:

1) Martyr's Day
2) Friendship Day
3) Valentine's Day

Write five lines about each of these days— why they are celebrated and what people normally do on those days.

TASK 3

Read the following paragraphs and answer the questions given below:

LITTLE BRAVE HEARTS

SHIVANI, ARIF AND ANURAG

On the morning of 18 November 1997, 11 year-old Shivani Sharma and her younger brother Jatin boarded their bus to go to school. Ten-year-old Mohammad Arif was also in the bus. The bus was packed much beyond its capacity. While crossing the Wazirabad bridge on the river Yamuna, the speeding bus overturned and breaking the iron railing on the bridge, fell into the river. Within moments the vehicle was filled with water. Trapped in between the seats, the students started screaming and made desperate attempts to get out. With immense effort Shivani and Arif managed to reach the window and break the glass panes. Thereafter they pulled out several students through the windows and helped them climb atop the roof of the bus safely. Fishermen rescued the children from there. Though she saved other children. Shivani could not save her brother Jatin. Fifteen-year-old Anurag, another schoolmate, travelling in a city bus just behind their ill-fated vehicle saw the accident. Without a moment's hesitation he jumped into the river. Braving the chilly water he ferried ten to twelve of his schoolmates to safety. Shivani, Arif and Anurag thus displayed exemplary courage and sense of duty in saving several lives.

YAMINI

Around 7 p.m. on 7 July 1997 some children were playing in a compound. Suddenly, seven-year-old Gaurav fell into a four-feet-deep ditch filled with coal-tar and gradually started sinking. While the other children fled, Yamini, acted swiftly. She grabbed Gaurav's hand and hair, thus preventing the young boy from sinking completely. However, despite intense efforts, she could not pull him out of the ditch. Realizing that she would not succeed in her mission. Yamini raised an alarm, but there was no one to hear her screams. The brave girl did not lose heart and held on to Gaurav firmly. After about an hour, a fireman, who was going towards the Nagarpalika office, heard her. Seeing Gaurav in danger, he collected some other people and with their help saved the little boy. Yamini's presence of mind and timely assistance saved Gaurav's life.

PRAMOD ARORA

On 4 November 1997, fourteen-year-old Pramod Arora, his mother and younger brother were returning to Nagpur from Nasik in a truck loaded with bricks. On the way, near Khumari, the truck overturned. Anticipating trouble, the driver jumped out from the window while Ali and the fifteen passengers were trapped under the bricks. Notwithstanding his injuries, Pramod managed to pull out his unconscious mother from the truck. Spotting his brother's red shirt, he retrieved him too. Displaying immense presence of mind and risking his life, Pramod lay down in the middle of the road. The idea worked and some persons travelling in a jeep came to his rescue. The injured were taken to a nearby medical centre for first aid and later to a hospital.

MOHAMMAD ASLAM

This incident occurred on 14 April 1998. A water pipe running parallel to a railway track in Rampur burst, causing the water to gush out and erode the soil beneath the railway track—thus forming a big hole under it. Md. Aslam knew this was dangerous. He looked around and noticed a red sock lying there. Tearing the sock, he made a flag by hoisting it on to a stick. Hearing the whistle of an approaching train from the other end, Aslam ran on to the track as fast as he could with the flag in his hand. There were tense moments. However, the train driver, noticing Aslam with the red flag, stopped the train approximately 500 feet away from the spot. Aslam's presence of mind and timely act thus saved several lives.

1. At what time and on which day did Gaurav fall into the ditch?

2. When did Shivani and Jatin board the bus to go to school?

3. When did the water pipe burst in Rampur?

4. When did Surendra fight with the dogs?

5. When did Pramod Arora return to Nagpur?

IT TRAVELLED **FOR** FIFTY-SIX YEARS!

Indicating Time and Duration: Prepositions of Time—for, since, ago

Read the folling and answer the questions given below:

Years Late

A postcard sent by a Dutch gas company during the Second World War has finally reached its destination—after sixty-two years.

The card addressed to Mr. N.H. Ter Kuile and dated 2 February 1943, was delivered to a house in the town of Zeggelt in Netherlands.

In the card, the Municipal Gas Factory asked Ter Kuile to report to counter 10 at the distribution office.

Postal officials could not explain the delay that began during Germany's wartime occupation of the Netherlands.

This letter had been travelling **since** ——————————————.

It had travelled **for** ——————————————.

It was sent —————————————— **ago.**

- **For** is used to refer to a **period** of time—to say **how long** some action took. It can be used with the simple past or present/past perfect tense.

- **Since** is used to say when some action/event began. It refers to a point of time. Since is used with the present/past perfect tense.
- **Ago** is used to say when a certain action/event happened in the past. It is used with the simple past tense form.

TASK 1

An Italian soldier lost his wallet in 1942. It was found in 1998 by a French builder who stumbled upon it while clearing the ruins of his house. A letter in the wallet provided the name of the owner, who is now seventy-eight years old.

(i) How many years ago was it lost? ------------------------------

(ii) The wallet had been missing since ------------------------------

(iii) It was missing for ------------------------------

(iv) The owner of the wallet must have been years old 56 years ago. ------------------------------

(v) The owner had lost his wallet since his ------------------------------ year.

TASK 2

Correct the errors in the following sentences and rewrite them. In some cases, you might have to change the tense.The first one is done for you.

1. I have been playing here for 9 o'clock in the morning.
   I have been playing here **since** 9 o'clock in the morning or I played here at 9 o'clock in the morning.

2. I've met him many years ago.

   ----

3. My friend came home 10 years back.

   ----

4. Mr. Naidu has been the Chief Minister of Andhra Pradesh since five years.

   ----

5. Azharuddin is playing cricket from 1983.

   ----

6. I have constructed my house in Bangalore ten years ago.

   ----

7. It has been raining for last evening.

   ----

8. Cricket was played in our country since many years.

   ----

9. I haven't met my childhood friends since a long time.

   ----

10. Dinosaurs were alive many years since.

TASK 3

Fill in the blanks with for, since or ago.

The city of Bombay consisted of seven islands a long time ________ This group of islands formed part of the kingdom of Ashoka in 273 BC. ________ Ashoka's death, these islands had been ruled by different Hindu rulers. In 1343, however, the Mohammedans of Gujarat took possession and these kinds ruled ________ two centuries. In 1534, the Portuguese took Bombay by force from the Mohammedans and they ruled ________ 128 years.

In 1662, the islands were given to the English king Charles II in dowry on his marriage to the Portuguese Princes Catherine of Braganza. About 300 years ________ in 1668 East India Company acquired the islands on lease for a sum of 10 pounds in gold per year.

________ 1998, it has been changed to Mumbai from Bombay.

LITTERING[1], SPITTING AND HONKING[2]

Gerunds

TIME PASS

dЄŞí ŞtylЄ

Indians are people with simple tastes. Here is a sample of a few of our favourite national pastimes.

- **Littering** is a popular activity in the cities. People do not think twice before dropping wrappers, plastic bags, banana peels and, of course, bus tickets on a public road. This has become a national sport at which we excel.
- **Spitting** is another favourite act which requires a special technique. Spitting is avoided at home, but happens from bus windows, round unsuspecting corners; and sometimes spit may land on your shoes, or on your clean white sari.
- **Honking** is the first thing that Indian drivers pick up. Usually, it is loud and for no reason at all. Instead of them getting bored in traffic jams and at red lights, drivers are entertained by these musical horns.

1. What are our favourite pastimes?

   ----

2. What are we fond of dropping on the road?

   ----

1 Littering: small pieces of rubbish that are left lying on the ground at public places.
2. Honking: the sound made by the horn of a vehicle.

3. Where is spitting done?

----

4. On what is spitting done?

----

5. What does every Indian driver pick up first?

The -ing form of the verb that functions like a noun is called a Gerund. As it functions like a noun, it can be

- in the subject position
  i. **Littering** is a national pastime.
  ii. **Swimming** is good for health.
  iii. **Travelling** makes me sick.

- in the object position
  i. I like **swimming.**
  ii. Prem enjoys **watching** horror films.

- in the complement position
  i. My favourite pastime is **swimming.**
  ii. The main problem in grammar is **understanding** the rules well.
  iii. The best thing in the morning is **having** a hot cup of coffee.

A complement in a sentence is the word/ phrase/ clause that comes after verbs like 'to be', 'to become', 'to turn', 'to change' that indicates a state or a change of state.

e.g. My brother is a doctor.
He became a doctor to serve the poor and the needy.

- after prepositions
  i. Can you come home after **finishing** your work?
  ii. I don't believe in **buying** expensive clothes.
  iii. We are so fond of **eating** spicy food.
  iv. Use this after **reading** the instructions carefully.

- after verbs like 'enjoy', 'adore', 'dislike', 'loathe', and 'can't stand'
  i. I enjoy **listening** to music
  ii. I dislike **reading** grammar books.
  iii. I loathe **learning** rules of grammar

- as a noun compound
  - i. a **diving** board
  - ii. a **swimming** pool
  - iii. a **writing** pad

TASK 1

Read the following advertisement:

Washing vessels with Rabeena keeps them bright and sparkling.

Write advertisements of a similar kind for the following five products/companies.

1. Singapore Airlines
   Flying ______________________

2. Water Guard (water purifier)
   Drinking ______________________

3. Santro Car
   Driving ______________________

4. Sunsilk Shampoo
   Washing hair ______________________
   Using ______________________

5. Archies comics
   Reading ______________________

TASK 2

Have you heard of Nisha Millet? Nisha Millet is a swimmer who has won many medals at important events. She was once asked what she loved and what she hated. This is what she said:

'I love **reading, chatting** with my friends, **listening** to heavy metal music. I love life, my family, friends and **SWIMMING**, of course.'

'I hate **fighting,** Hindi music, cricket and eggs!'

Make a survey of the favourite hobbies (what they enjoy doing) of five of your friends. Place them in a scale of 1-10 (the least preferred to the most preferred). For example

Names	1	2	3	4	5	6	7	8	9	0

Write about the most preferred hobby and the least preferred one. Use gerunds wherever possible.

Read and enjoy this joke:

Sumo **wrestling** is survival of the fattest!

TASK 3

Look up a dictionary for the meanings of the word 'surf'. Like many words of English, the word 'surf' too has two meanings.

surf: to spend time visiting the websites e.g By **surfing** the net everyday, one can get information on employment opportunities abroad.
surf: to ride on a wave by standing on or by lying on a board e.g. I love **surfing** on the ocean.

Look at the table given below.

SURFING THE NET	SURFING ON THE SEA

chatting with people	**riding** on the waves
e-mailing to friends	**balancing** on the board
reading interesting bits of information	**floating** horizontally
browsing the net	not **dropping** in on a wave
copying files	**keeping** in contact with the board
saving information	**surfing** with a buddy
downloading software	
storing on a floppy	
playing a CD	

The two tables list some of the thing you do when you surf a net or when you surf on the sea. Can you write a paragraph using the gerunds given in the two boxes?

....

....

....

....

....

....

TASK 4

Read the following item on the 'Evils of Begging'.

EVILS OF BEGGING

Begging is a long established custom in India, and **giving** alms has religious sanction. Hence, it is not easy to make people see that it is an evil that should be regulated by law and discouraged by the public.
Are all the beggars really poor and deserve help? Is alms **giving** the best way of **helping** the poor?
Poverty is not helped by casual alms **giving.** Only a systematic organization of charitable relief can be effective. To give money to a beggar may ease the giver's conscience, but it does not solve the problem of poverty, instead, it intensifies it.

Write a similar item on the 'Evils of Smoking' or 'Evils of Copying in an Examination', <u>using gerunds where possible.</u>

You could use the clues given below.

Smoking : bad for health—can cause cancer, heart ailments. buying cigarettes—wasteful expenditure. stop smoking—try chewing gum instead.

Copying : is a malpractice because it's against the rules—Does not show your true knowledge. Studying well is important. Writing what you know—better than copying. Perhaps setting of paper could be different—more open book pattern questions—to prevent copying.

ON BECOMING INTOXICATED

Participial Clauses

Read the following:

Being hungry, a dung beetle went out in search of food. He came to a place where a gang of dacoits had recently feasted. **Seeing a few drops of wine on a leaf,** the beetle lapped[1] it up. **Then becoming intoxicated,** he swaggered[2] back to the ball of dung in which he lived. The dung **being moist,** gave way a little. The beetle was thrilled.

'The world can't bear my weight', he shouted. 'Is there anyone here more powerful than me?'

An elephant, **happening to come by at that time,** was disgusted by the smell of the dung. So, he turned away. The beetle, **thinking that he had turned away out of fear of him,** yelled:

'Why are you running away? Come back and fight and let us see who is stronger. Are we not . . .' He never finished. **Picking up a big piece of dung,** the elephant dropped it on him, **knocking him senseless.**

1. Why did the beetle go out in search of food?

2. Why did he swagger back?

---

1. **lapped:** to drink quickly by licking something up.
2. **swaggered:** to walk in a way that shows you are important, or to act in that way.

3. The moist dung gave way. Why?

4. How did the elephant show his anger?

5. What was the result?

Two or more sentences can be combined using a participial clause.

Participial clauses answer the questions:

Why? When? How? or On what condition ?

e.g. **Being hungry**, the beetle went out in search of food. (Why?)

Feeling bored, I walked out of the theatre (Why?)

Before going to bed, I say my prayers. (When?)

My son loves to eat chips **while watching the television** (When?)

Dropping a huge piece of dung on the beetle, the elephant knocked him out. **(How?)**

By running at great speed, I managed to get into the bus. (How?)

If invited, I'll go for the party (On what condition?)

If caught copying in the examination, you will be suspended **(On what condition?)**

A participial clause has a verb (without tense) in the **-ing** or **-en (or -ed) form.**

e.g. He was angry ——> **Being angry,**

I am invited ———> **If invited,**

The difference between a gerund and a participle is that a gerund is always **nominal** in nature whereas a participle is adverbial in nature. This means that the gerund can occur wherever a noun phrase can occur, namely, in the subject, object, object of a **preposition** and in the complement position. A participial occurs only where an adverbial or adjectival occurs, namely, in the adjunct position.

TASK 1

Combine the two underlined sentences or clauses using a participial clause.

The first one is done for you.

After she came home, she switched on the television.

On coming home, she switched on the television

1. **A man had trouble getting sleep at night. He went to a doctor.**

   Having - - - - - - - - -

2. **When the doctor heard his problem, he prescribed some extra strong sleeping pills for him.**

   On hearing - - - - - - - - —

3. **'If the pills are taken at night, they will cure your illness'**, the doctor said.

   If taken - - - - - - - -

4. **The man took the pills on Sunday night. He slept well** and awoke before the alarm rang.

   On taking - - - - - - - -

5. **He arrived at the office. He said to his boss, 'I didn't have any trouble getting up this morning'.**

   On arriving - - - - - - - -

6. **His boss heard this. He roared—'That's fine. But where were you on Monday and Tuesday?'**

   Hearing this, - - - - - - - -

TASK 2

Underline the participial clauses in the sentences given below. Then draw an arrow to indicate the noun or pronoun it modifies. The first one is done for you.

1. Jane Goodall, recognized as a chimp champ, has devoted most of her life to studying chimpanzees.

   -

2. Having lived in Gombe National Park in Tanzania for many years, Jane understands the behaviour of chimpanzees very well.

----

3. Jane gives the chimps names, drawn from friends and family.

----

4. Her research, explaining everything about chimps, is extremely interesting.

----

5. Watching their behaviour carefully, Jane observed that the chimps were like humans.

----

6. When the chimp 'Flint's' mother died, he sat for days near the body, hoping for her to get up.

----

7. Not having eaten anything for many days due to his sorrow, Flint too collapsed and died at the same spot.

----

8. Jane has written many articles, describing the plight of chimps now.

----

9. Frequently caught by poachers for sale to circuses, zoos and for medical research, chimps are decreasing in number.

----

10. Recognizing the need to protect them, the U.S Wildlife service has listed them as an endangered species.

TASK 3

Combine each pair of sentences using a participial clause. The first one is done for you.

1. **I saw a car with the red-coloured 'L' sign at the back. I explained to my young niece that the driver was a learner.**
   On seeing a car with the red-coloured 'L' sign at the back, I explained to my young niece that the driver was a learner.

   ----

2. Some time later, she saw her two-year-old sister walking unsteadily. She asked. 'Uncle, can't we paint an "L" on baby's back?'

   ----

3. I heard this. I laughed.

   ----

4. Two men sat down on the top deck of a bus. They began chatting to each other.

   ----

5. An inspector examined their tickets. He asked them where they had boarded the bus.

   ----

6. They heard this question. They answered: 'Downstairs'.

   ----

7. A farmer's son had been educated at boarding schools and in a city university. He had no knowledge or interest in the land.

   ----

8. He did not know what to do. He asked his father for advice.

   ----

9. His father wanted his son to stay in the village. So he said: 'Till the soil'.

   ----

10. The son did not understand this. He asked: 'Till the soil what?'

TASK 4

Misplaced/Dangling participial clauses

When two sentences are combined by using a participial clause, the subject can be omitted from one of them if it is the **same.**

e.g. I got up from bed. I rushed to the bathroom.

Getting up from bed, I rushed to the bathroom.

However, if the subjects are different, they cannot be omitted.

The bus was crowded. I had to stand.

Being crowded, I had to stand (X)

The bus being crowded, I had to stand (ü)

If the participial clause does not have a word to modify, it is known as a **dangling modifier.**

e.g. Being crowded, I had to stand.

In this sentence, the participial 'Being crowded' does not have a noun or pronoun to refer to. This is a dangling modifier.

A **misplaced modifier** is when the word that the participial clause modifies is placed so far that the meaning is unclear.

e.g. Hiding under the bed, I saw the frightened dog.

Here, the participial clause 'Hiding under the bed' refers to the dog and not to me. However, as it is placed very far from the word it modifies, the meaning is unclear.

Read the following sentences and correct the errors (if any)

1. The college examinations were over a week ago. I began cleaning my locker in the staff room.
Being over a week ago, I began cleaning my locker in the staff room.

----

2. The college was closed. The students were missing.
On being closed, the students were missing.

----

3. I searched for my class file.
I found the projects of my students.
While searching for my class file, I found the projects of my students.

----

4. Roopa's project on wildlife was on top of the pile. I looked at it carefully.
Being on top, I looked at it carefully.

----

5. Roopa was naughty. She had made every animal's face resemble a teacher in the school!
Being naughty, Roopa had made every animal's face resemble a teacher in the school!

----

6. I was irregular. Roopa had made me a dinosaur—an extinct animal!
Being irregular, Roopa had made me a dinosaur—an extinct animal!

Read and enjoy this joke.

A patient, **having undergone treatment for a month in a hospital**, received the following note from the doctor:

'Good news, Mrs.Sharma. A team of doctors think you're strong enough to see your bill!'

TASK 5

Rewrite the following letter using participial clauses wherever possible.

Me and Myself

Waking up in the morning and getting ready for college is my biggest problem. That is why I wait for holidays. My idea of a perfect getaway would be an island. An island with a small cabin just for me, with electricity, a fully stocked refrigerator, shelves full of storybooks. A soft bed and a television set. I would get up late, cook, and watch television. Evenings will be for swimming, fishing and lying on the sands. I would read late into the night and go to sleep. Mealtimes would be special because I'd cook my own food and have a delicious dessert after every meal! What a holiday it would be with no one to tell me what to do, eating whenever I want, going to bed late and watching TV to my heart's content.

Waking up in the morning and getting ready for college is my biggest problem. That is why I wait for holidays.

——— (Use 'being' instead of 'is')

IF YOU **SEE** THE WATER RECEDE QUICKLY, **RUN** TOWARD HIGHER GROUND

Expressing Cause and Effect or Outcome of Events: The Open Condition

A tsunami is caused by an underwater earthquake. We experienced a tsunami in December 2004 in our country and in some neighbouring ones. This is what the tsunami experts say:

If you see the water recede quickly and unexpectedly from a beach (this is called drawback), **run toward higher ground or inland**—there may be a tsunami coming. Also, **if you are on the coast and there is an earthquake**, it may have caused a tsunami, so **run toward higher ground or inland**. Some beaches have tsunami warning sirens—do not ignore them. The first wave in a tsunami is often not the largest; **if you experience an abnormally-huge wave, go inland quickly**—even bigger waves could be coming soon.

These sentences tell us of what the outcome should be if the condition mentioned in the 'if' clause is met.

If clause	**Main clause**
If you see the water recede quickly and unexpectedly from a beach,	run toward higher ground or inland.
If you are on the coast and there is an earthquake,	run toward higher ground or inland.
If you experience an abnormally-huge wave,	go inland quickly.

The 'if' clause introduces a condition (something that may or may not happen). It usually comes before the main clause. The verbs in both the 'if' clause and the main clause are in the present tense. This is also known as an **open condition.**

TASK 1

Given below is a list of essential items to be taken if you go on a trip. Write fifteen sentences using the 'if' clause to describe what you have to take.

e.g. If you go on a trip, you must take some iodine pills to purify the water.

TASK 2

GUESS THE COUNTRY

We know that if you are in the land of the rising sun, you are in Japan.

Do you know the answers to these?

1. Land of the white elephant

2. Land of the midnight sun

3. Land of morning calm

4. Land of cakes

5. Land of thousand lakes

6. Land of thousand islands

7. Land of the golden pagoda

8. Land of dykes

9. Land of wood and water

Write these as 'if' clauses.

Answers:
1. Thailand
2. Norway
3. Korea
4. Scotland
5. Finland
6. Indonesia
7. Myanmar
8. Holland
9. Jamaica

TASK 3

Here is a problem letter by a boy who wants to know why his songbird doesn't sing and the reply. Read this and answer the questions.

The Problem

My dad bought me a songbird, a couple of months ago. But ever since it's been with me, there hasn't been a peep out of it. Help!

Harish, Mumbai

The expert's reply

In many species, only the male bird sings . . . and yours could be female.

Songbirds stop singing when they are moulting. See if your bird is beginning to moult.

In the wild, birds often sing to mark their territory and to attract mates. A caged bird could be lonely and scared and far to depressed to sing. Birds sing when they are happy. They love flying across the blue sky when the sun is shining. They love flitting from tree to tree to check out a fruit here or a flower there. So, how can you expect a caged bird to be cheerful? Tell me, if someone were to put you in a small cage and leave you in some corner of a strange house, far away from your friends and family, would you burst into song?

1. What could be the main reason for the bird not singing? (Use an 'if' clause)
2. What could be the second reason? (Use an 'if' clause)
3. If a bird sings in the wild, ______________________________ or ______________________________ (Give the two reasons)
4. If the bird doesn't sing, how is he?
5. When does the bird sing?
6. How does a bird feel if it is caged?
7. How will you feel if you are caged?

TASK 4

Emergency management.

You read at the beginning of this unit about what should be done if there is a sign of a tsunami. Do you know what should be done **if there is an earthquake**?

I. Match the following.

1. If **INDOORS,**	pull to the side of the road as quickly as possible, but keep away from overhead hazards such as trees, buildings, utility poles and lines, signs, and bridges. Stay in the vehicle until the shaking stops.
2. If you're in a **THEATRE OR STADIUM,**	do not rush for exits. If outdoors, stay outdoors. Move to an open area away from trees, buildings, utility poles and lines, or signs.

3. If in a **VEHICLE** — stay indoors. Move away from windows that may break and furniture or large objects that could fall over. Take cover under a table, bench or desk and hold on, or go to an interior wall or hallway. Expect fire alarm and sprinkler systems to activate.

4. If you're in a **CROWDED ROOM OR PUBLIC PLACE,** — stay in your seat or get under it if possible, and protect your head with your arms. Do not try to leave until the shaking is over.

B. Find out from some source about what should be done **if there is a fire?**

C. What should be done **if there is a severe storm?**

D. What should be done **if there is a flood?**

IF I GOT A HOLIDAY, I WOULD GO TO A COLD PLACE

Talking About Imaginary Situations and Their Consequences: Use of Would to Indicate Improbable Conditions

Cooling Off in the Arctic

Dust, Pollution noise and traffic. Ah! I'm tired of it all. The blazing sun makes it even worse. My getaway would probably be to a nice, cold place like the Arctic. The very thought of it makes me sit up.

I would go there in a helicopter and stay there for a fortnight or so. I would stay with the Eskimos in an igloo. I would watch the midnight sun stand all day long in the sky. Of course, not to forget the seals and their antics. Away from the busy and dusty city, I would borrow one of the Eskimos sleigh and have a whopping ride.

Yes! The Arctic would indeed be a haven where one could rejoice in the coolness and purity of air. Hmm . . . that place would be paradise. Alas! There's so much that separates Dream and Reality

The girl writing this passage would like to do a number of things. What are they?

She **would** go to a cold place like the Arctic.
She **would** go there in a helicopter.
She **would** stay with the Eskimos in an igloo.
She **would** watch the midnight sun.
She **would** watch the seals and their antics.
She **would** borrow a sleigh and have a ride.

Look at these two sentences:

If I **took** a holiday	I **would** go to the Arctic.
If I **went** to America	I **would** meet Bill Clinton.

In this condition, the 'if' clause is in the past tense and refers to an unlikely event. The main clause too has the verb in the past tense.

TASK 1

Where would you like to go and what would you like to do if you had a dream holiday?

TASK 2

A World Tour

My holiday would be a fabulous one. My day would begin at a hotel in Japan. I would love to receive the early rays in the land of the rising sun. I would take a dip in a pool of course, of hot water. Then I will be off to China where I would break my fast with some delicious noodles. Afternoon would be time for lunch and learning. I would laze about in the armoury museum in England to satisfy my appetite for weapons. For lunch some steaming chicken soup would be enough.

Evening means fun, which means the beaches of California. Dinner would be at the largest restaurant in Singapore and then off to a dreamy sleep.

What a day! Really a holiday worth dreaming about. Wait . . . I forgot to visit Mauritius! Maybe, next time . . .

Read this letter. List what the writer would do if he/she had a holiday.

i) in the morning

----

ii) in the afternoon

----

iii) in the evening

TASK 3

Here is an announcement of prizes to be won in a competition.

10 Weekly Draw
Prizes :
1st Prize : Bajaj Scooter
2nd Prize : BPL Washing Machine
(3) 3rd Prize : Kenstar Mixie
(4) 4th Prize : Titan Wrist Watch

23 Festival Draw
Prizes:
1st Prize : Fiat Siena Car
(2) 2nd Prize : BPL Washing Machine
(20) 3rd Prize : Titan Wrist Watch

Bumper Draw : Rs. 1,00,000/- worth Gold Necklace set and many more attractive prizes.

You are dreaming about the various prizes. Say what you would do.

i) if you won the 1st prize.

----

ii) if you won the 2nd prize.

----

iii) if you won the 3rd prize.

----

iv) if you won the 4th prize.

----

v) if you won the bumper prize of Rs. 1,00,000/- worth Gold Necklace set.

TASK 4

> If I were alone in a far off land.
> I would live peacefully and
> I would watch television for hours.
> In my own room full of flowers.
> If I were alone in a far off land.
> I would live as I want,
> I would not study and
> I would watch cricket for hours.

Write a paragraph on what you would do if you were:

a) a fierce Alsatian dog.

----

b) the principal of your school.

----

c) a famous actor or actress

IF SHE **HAD SCOLDED** ME, I **WOULDN'T HAVE BEEN** A THIEF

Talking About Impossible Situations and Their Consequences: Use of the Past Perfect in Impossible Conditions

A boy once stole a book from one of his schoolfellows. He brought it home to his mother, who was happy at his heroic deed.

When the boy grew up, he began to steal other things, jewels and money. And once, caught in the act of robbery, he murdered someone. Thus he was taken to jail and ordered to be hanged.

As the jailers were taking him to the gallows, he saw his mother weeping and wailing and beating her breasts. He begged the officers to allow her to speak to him. So they let him talk to his mother.

As he drew near his mother's ear, he bit the lobe hard with his teeth.

At this she cried out with pain, and the crowd joined her in shouting at the unnatural son.

'The rogue!' they said, 'he is not content with the crimes he has committed. He has bitten his own mother's ear.'

The thief replied, 'It is she who is the cause of my ruin. **If she had scolded me for stealing my school fellow's book in the beginning, I would never have grown up to be a thief at all.'**

The boy says: 'If she had scolded me, I wouldn't have been a thief'. It refers to something that was not done in the past and its consequence. This is an **impossible condition.** An impossible condition is formed by the use of the past perfect tense in the 'if' clause + would/could/might + perfect tense in the main clause.

e.g.: If I had won the prize, I would have had a car.

(But I haven't won the prize. So I don't have a car!)

TASK 1

List five things that the boy might have become/been if his mother had corrected him.

e.g. If his mother had corrected him, he could have become a police officer.

1. ____________________

2. ____________________

3. ____________________

4. ____________________

5. ____________________

TASK 2

The boy in the story was caught by the police and jailed. He had become a thief because his mother had not scolded him earlier. Imagine you are the boy and write a letter to your friend expressing your feelings of anger and regret. You could begin like this:

Mumbai
21 October 1999

Dear Vivek,

You must have read in the newspaper about me. I am in jail now for crimes that I committed. If my mother had helped me, I would - - - - - - - -

If I had not committed these crimes - - - - -

If only - - - - - - - -

THE CAT **ASKED** AND THE MOUSE **REPLIED**

Reporting Statements and Questions

Conversation
Rose Flyeman

'Mousie, Mousie,
Where is your little wee housie?
'Here is the door,
Under the floor,'
Said Mousie, Mousie.
'Mousie, Mousie,
May I come into your housie?'
'You can't get in
You have to be thin',
Said Mousie, Mousie,
'Mousie, mousie,
Won't you come out of your housie?'
'I'm sorry to say.
I'm busy all day,' said Mousie, Mousie

Observe the following changes

Questions

Direct speech	**Indirect speech**
'Where is your little wee housie?'	The cat asked the mousie where his little wee housie was.
'May I come into your housie?'	The cat wondered if he could go into his house
'Won't you come out of your housie?'	The cat enquired whether the mousie would come out of his house.

Statements

Direct speech	**Indirect speech**
'Here is the door under the floor'	The mouse replied that the door of his house was under the floor.
'You can't get in. You have to be thin'.	The mouse warned that the cat could not get in because he had to be thin.
'I'm sorry to say I'm busy all day'	The mouse apologized for being busy all day.

Note the following changes:

- The quotation marks are omitted in indirect speech.
- The tense of the verb changes.
  simple present simple past.
  e.g. is ———> was
  can ———> could
  will ———> would
- simple past ———> past perfect

Reena said :
'I saw a movie yesterday' — Reena said that she **had seen** a movie yesterday.

- Present continuous ———> Past continuous
  'I am singing.' — 'He said that he was singing'

- A statement is reported by using verbs like **said, reported, told, informed admitted, apologised, warned.**
- A question is reported by using verbs like **asked, enquired, wondered** - - - - -
- If the question is a yes/no one, the indirect speech will have if / whether.

e.g. 'Do you like cricket?' asked Manoj.
Manoj asked if / whether I liked cricket.
If the question is a wh–one, the indirect speech will begin with that wh–word.

e.g. 'What is your name?,' asked my teacher.
My teacher asked me what my name was.

TASK 1

Who said these famous words after India's victory in the 1983 World Cup match?

Match the following

	What they said	Person
i)	'My slogan is: India can do it.'	Ajay Jadeja
ii)	'I was barely 10 plus so I don't remember too much'	Javagal Srinath
iii)	'I still remember Amarnath getting Holding lbw and the tears in my eyes'	Anil Kumble
iv)	'I watched every ball of the match'	Indira Gandhi
v)	'I idolised Kapil paaji right from my childhood. To me, he was the hero of our world cup triumph.'	Sachin Tendulkar
vi)	'Even before we started the match, I had this firm belief that India would emerge winners'	Nayan Mongia

Report these statements. The first one is done for you :

Indira Gandhi, P.M. said that her slogan was that India could do it.

Answer: 1. Indira Gandhi 2. Sachin Tendulkar 3. Anil Kumble 4. Nayan Mongia 5. Javagal Srinath

TASK 2

Read the following poem:

My Child

Oh! My child, cuddled by my side,
The hands so small, yet so lovely;
I kissed, I held it close to my heart
And said. 'My child, I live for you.'

He grew, my child, brilliant and smart:
Naughty he was, but loved me too.
I dreamed, that someday he'll make me proud;
He told me, 'Ma, I'll be worthy of you.'

At school, my boy, he always stood first;
To send him to learn, I knew not what,
I borrowed, I sold and pawned all I had.
He promised, 'Ma, I'll live up to your dreams.'

Now he is married, with children sweet,
With property and money and status too.
He tells me I am but an old fool:
'Alas! my child, I love you still.'

'My child, I live for you'

Report what the mother said to her child when he was a baby ('I live for you')

i) 'I'll be worthy of you.'
Report what the boy said to his mother when young.

ii) 'I'll live up to your dreams.'
Report what the mother says to her son even now.

iii) 'I love you still'.

TASK 3

Read the following passage: and rewrite the underlined sentences in indirect speech.

The umpire's finger went up, the other team cheered and 10-year old Jim's heart sank!

This was his third cricket match.

Walking back, he thought, 'This is my third match and all three times I've been out for a duck, I'm no good. I'm useless. I'll resign. No, no need to do that they'll surely remove me from the team!'

'Bad luck Jim, but don't worry there's always a next time,' said Mr Jones, the coach.

'No, I'm just a bad player, please don't chuck me out, I'll resign,' said Jim.

'Look Jim, we will not remove you from the team and you will not resign. I've got a little story to tell you,' replied Mr Jones.

'I started playing cricket when I was about 11. With hard work I managed to get into my class team. I played in four matches and then was removed as I was out for a duck in all four matches. Then after a long time I managed to get into the team again. I played two matches in which I didn't score. Then in my third match I could hardly believe I scored a half-century and I was the highest scorer. Since then I always played well and I was never removed from the class team. I even played for the school.'

'And now you coach and inspire many boys to play cricket' said Jim. 'I swear I'll never resign from the team.'

'Good boy, I'm proud of you. Not only me, but even great players have become great only because they never gave up,' said the coach.

Rewrite the underlined sentences as indirect speech.

e.g. 'This is my third match and all three times. I've been out duck.'

Jim realized that **that was his** third match and all three times **he had been** out for a duck.

Begin the sentences as given:

1) 'I'm no good.'
Jim believed ____________________

2) 'There's always a next time,' said Mr.Jones.
Mr Jones consoled Jim by saying ____________

3) 'I started playing cricket when I was about eleven.'
Mr Jones said ______________________

4) 'With hard work I managed to get into my class team.'
Mr Jones noted ______________________

5) 'I played in four matches and then was removed from the team as I was out for a duck in all four matches.'
Mr Jones confessed ______________

6) 'Then after a long time I managed to get into the team again.'
Mr Jones added ______________________

7) 'I played two matches in which I didn't score.'
Mr Jones admitted ______________________

8) 'In my third match I could hardly believe I scored a half-century and was the highest scorer.'
Mr Jones continued excitedly ______________

9) 'Since then I always played well and I was never removed from the class team.'
Mr Jones concluded ______________________

10) 'I'll never resign from the team.'
Jim promised ______________________

11) 'Not only me, but even great players have become great only because they never gave up,' said the coach.
The coach, Mr Jones reminded Jim ______________

I INSTRUCT YOU TO

Reporting Commands, Requests and Pieces of Advice

Reported / Indirect Speech: Imperatives

Read the following poem:

You are going out to tea today,
So mind how you behave;
Let all accounts I have of you
Be pleasant ones, I crave.
Don't spill your tea or gnaw your bread
And don't tease one another;
And Tommy mustn't talk too much, or quarrel with his brother.
Say 'If you please' and 'Thank you' come home at eight o'clock'
And, Fanny, pray be careful that you do not tear your frock.
Now, mind your manners, children five, attend to what I say,
And then perhaps I'll let you go
Again another day.

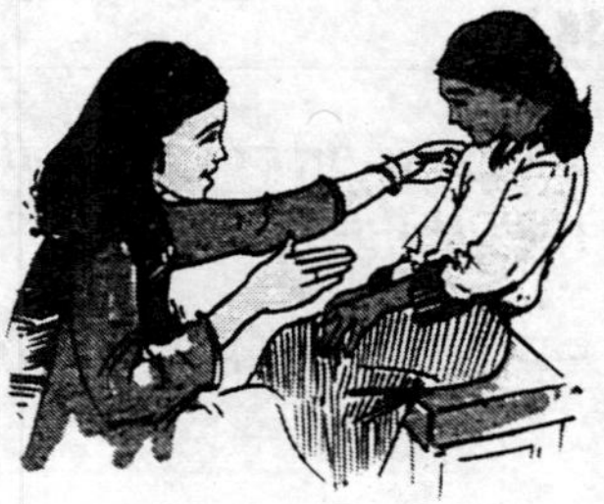

In this poem, the lady **instructs the children not to spill their** tea or **gnaw their bread.**

She also **asks them not to tease one another.**

She **orders** Tommy **not to talk too much or quarrel with his brother.**

The lady **instructs them to come home at eight o'clock.**

She **asks Fanny to be careful about her frock.**

She finally requests **them to mind their manners and attend to what she says.**

- **Indirect speech: Commands and Requests**
  Observe the following changes :

Direct speech (command or request)	**Indirect speech**
'Close the door'	My friend **ordered** me **to** close the door.
'Pass the salt please'	Sheela **requested** me **to** pass the salt.

- Commands, requests and pieces of advice are reported using the following frame :

My friend/she ________ him to ________

The verbs commonly used to report commands are **tell, warn, command, order, instruct** etc.

The verbs commonly used to report requests are **request, ask**

The verbs commonly used to report pieces of advice are **advice, tell** ________

TASK 1

It is your first day at college. Your principal tells you what you can or can't do in college. Report this to your parents. (Use the clues in brackets)

e.g. Our principal has **ordered us to be** in college by 8.30 a.m.

i) ____________________ (warn—punishment if late)

ii) ____________________ (instruct—go to class after assembly)

iii) ____________________ (tell—bring our parents every Saturday for a parent-teacher meeting)

iv) ____________________ (ask—take part in extracurricular activities)

v) ____________________ (advise—study well and bring honour and name to the college)

TASK 2

Read the following piece of advice to parents on bringing up children.

> **'Your children are not your children.**
> They are the sons and daughters of Life's longing for itself.
> And it is your responsibility **to pass on the torch of civilization to them.**
> **Teach them to think.**
> To wonder, **to dream.** To meet triumph and disaster, equally.
> Teach them the difference between flattery and praise.
> Teach them the joy of a sunset.
> The joy of sharing.
> The joy of discovering the unknown.
> **More than anything else,**
> **Teach them to walk tall.'**

Write this passage as a report beginning:

Parents are advised to teach their children . . .

- -

- -

- -

- -

- -

TASK 3

Read the following proverbs. Rewrite them as indirect statements. The first one is done for you.

1. Make hay while the sun shines. This proverb tells us

   -

2. An early bird catches the worm. This proverb asks us

   -

3. A bird in hand is worth two in the bush. This proverb instructs us

   -

4. Early to bed and early to rise makes a man healthy, wealthy and wise.
   This proverb tells us

   -

5. Slow and steady wins the race. This proverb advises us

   -

6. United we stand, divided we fall. This proverb requests us

   -

7. An idle man is a devil's workshop. This proverb warns us

   -

THEIR FATE ONLY THE U.N.CAN DECIDE

How to Highlight Something: Inversion for Focusing

Read the following poem:

The troubled heights
Kargil, Kargil burning bright
In between two nuclear heights
A sorry state it is both sides
Who once constituted a country, wide
Now each is thirsty for the other's blood
Causing civilians at the borders to flee
As both countries refuse to abide
Their fate only the U.N. can decide.

- When we want to draw the attention of the reader (or hearer) to particular parts of a sentence, we use certain methods to highlight them. One of them is **inversion or change in word order.**

  e.g. Only the U.N. can decide **their fate** (normal word order).
  Their fate only the U.N. can decide (inverted order, to draw the reader's attention to the fate of the two countries).

TASK 1

Look at the following sentences:

Never has he tried to help me.

No sooner did he see the plane crash, he ran to the site.

Under no circumstances should small children ride scooters.

In these sentences, an adverbial phrase is taken to the beginning of the sentence for focussing.

Inversion

Adverbial phrase	first part of the verb	subject	main verb
Never	has	he	tried
No sooner	did	he	see

Complete each of the following sentences in such a way that it means exactly the same as the sentence given before it.

A father one day asked his two daughters: 'What is the sweetest thing in the world?' 'Sugar,' said the older girl. 'Salt', said his younger daughter.

i) The father had not heard a sillier reply than this.
Never ______________________________

ii) When he heard the reply, he became angry and threw her out of the house.
No sooner than ______________________

iii) 'You will not enter my house again', he shouted
Under no circumstance ____________________

The younger daughter went to the forest. A prince who had come to hunt saw her.

iv) The girl was very beautiful. The prince wanted to marry her.
So beautiful ______________________

The girl and the prince got married. They had a feast in the palace. The girl invited her father for the feast. She served all the dishes without salt.

v) As soon as her father started eating, he realized how important salt was.
Hardly had ______________________

TASK 2

Read the following passage and answer the questions:

Dr. Ani Mal was a famous veterinary surgeon but **a careless surgeon was he!** He left things like forceps and scissors in the body of the animal he operated upon.

One day, he had to operate on an elephant. Throughout the operation, the nurse, a small but stern faced woman kept telling him, **'Under no circumstances** should you leave an instrument behind this time.'

Finally the surgery was over. **Never had the doctor been more pleased** with the way he had handled the delicate operation.

'Didn't leave anything behind this time, did I, nurse?' he asked as he washed his hands at the sink.

No sooner had he completed this sentence than he realized that though all his instruments were there, the nurse was missing!

1. Dr. Ani Mal was a famous doctor but——————————————!
2. What did the nurse keep telling him during the operation?
3. Was the doctor pleased with the operation?
4. When did the doctor realize that the nurse was missing?
5. What do you think had happened to the nurse?

TASK 3

Make a short speech on the topic given below.

Use under no circumstances, never - - - - , rarely - - not only - - - - - - but also *for emphasis.*
Use the clues given below.

Is television viewing good or bad for children?

1. Can learn new things but not good for the eyes.
2. Makes learning interesting—but children don't read books.
3. Can watch games and learn about them — waste of time.

- For special emphasis, we often use a sentence beginning with:

It is/ was ——————which/ that ——————emphasized word/ phrase

e.g. It is dancing that I like, not singing.
It was my mother who opened the door.

- Another way to emphasize is by using a 'what . . . is/ was . . .' construction.

e.g. What Saleem managed to do was cheat Mohammad
What I like most is cricket.

TASK 4

Using the following clues, write a newspaper report. Use 'It is....'or 'What...' to highlight the underlined phrases.

At 1:30 in the night of December 31, 1999, Vijay and Vivek—two college students–returning from New Year Eve party–driving on the highway. Something made them stop their car–was a lady in a white saree. Lady wished them 'Happy New Year' and asked them the way to Ashok Nagar. They gave her the directions. Vijay tried to start the car. The car wouldn't start. He turned back to see if the lady was there–lady vanished–a ghost that Vijay and Vivek had seen. What Vijay and Vivek do–leave car, take taxi and go home.

Gwalior
3.1.2000

It was at 1:30 in the night of December 31, 1999 that Vijay and Vivek, two college students were . . .

TASK 5

Read the passage given below and complete the answers.

On top of the world

It was at 11:30 a.m on 29 May 1953, that Edmund Hillary, a beekeeper from New Zealand, and Tenzing Norgay, a Nepalese mountain climber from the Sherpa community, became the first human beings to reach the top of the world. What they had done was conquer the 8848 m high Himalayan peak Mount Everest!

1. **Who** were the two men to reach the top of the world?

It was --

2. When did they reach the top of the world?

It was --

3. What had they done?

What they had done ----------------------------------

4. Who was Edmund Hillary and where was he from?

----

5. Who was Tenzing Norgay and where was he from?

----

6. Do you like mountain climbing?

It is -------------------------- that I like.

PART 2

LETTER WRITING

In this age of correspondence through e-mail, fax and mobile, letter writing is gradually fading away. But nobody can entirely do away with this form of communication, which should be cultivated by everyone. So let us learn the art of writing letters.

Although there are different kinds of letters—personal, business, official, etc.—the basic format in all letter-writing is the same. We shall now discuss this format in some detail.

THE FORMAT

- **The Heading**
- **Salutation**
- **The Subject**
- **The Body of the Letter**
- **Salutation with corresponding subscription**
- **The Signature**

- ***The Heading***

This heading carries the writer's name, address and date, usually given in the following manner, in the left and right-hand corners of the paper.

R.K. Ramaratnam
35 Minto Road
New Delhi 110001

19 April 2004

Note: Ordinarily, the above heading is already printed in case of an official letter on top, in the left-hand corner. The date however, may be written in two different ways — (a) 19 April 2004 or (b) 19-4-2004. The former way is, however, more commonly used.

(Don't use *No.* before 35 Minto Road, and no comma after 35)

- **Salutation**

Each letter should begin from the left hand side and should be followed by a comma (and no such other punctuation mark as colon (:) or dash (–). Of course, the form of salutation will differ according to the person addressed.

Given below is a list of the form of address in each case:

An unmarried woman	—	Miss Usha Kapur, Miss K. Bhasker
A married woman	—	Mrs. Veena Shouria, Mrs. Sunanda Rao
Nowadays, the form **Ms.** is used for both married and unmarried women.		
A married or unmarried man	—	Mr. Srinivas Reddy, Mr. S. Reddy or Shri B.P. Marathey
A military officer	—	Colonel A. Hussain or Col. A. Hussain
A doctor (law, medicine, literature, etc.)	—	Dr. G. Chary
A clergyman	—	Rev. T. Samuel or The Rev. T. Samuel (Rev. is the short form of Reverend)
A young girl	—	Miss Sushma Saini or Miss Anusuya Kumar
A young boy	—	Master Taru Singh or Master T. Singh
A Member of Parliament	—	Shri Kuldip Sood, M.P.

(Remember that if a letter is to be forwarded to another address, you should write *Please Forward* in the top left-hand corner.)
Remember that C/o (care of) accompanies a person's name (not his place of residence). e.g. C/o Mrs. J. Sarin

Also remember that no full stop is placed at the end of an address.

- **The Subject**

Remember that in the case of a business or official letter, it is always helpful to mention the subject (of the body of the letter) after the salutation:

Dear Sir,

<u>Supply of Spare Parts</u>

- **The body of the letter**

This part of the letter stating the matter should be presented in paragraphs. The phrasing should be simple, direct and supported by relevant details. (see examples given subsequently in this chapter).

- **Salutation with corresponding subscription**

Sir,	—	Yours truly,
Dear Sir,	—	Yours faithfully,
Dear Mr. Hussain,	—	Yours sincerely,
My dear Miss Ansari,	—	Yours very sincerely,
Dear Sunder,	—	Yours ever,

Darling Mother, — Fondest love from (or Your loving son)
My dear Uncle, — Yours affectionately,

(Remember that you should not write *Your's sincerely*—the correct expression is *Yours sincerely,)*

- **The Signature**

You should always make your signature legible. And it should be written in hand even if the rest of the letter has been done on a typewriter/ computer. Leave adequate margin on both sides to make the letter as presentable as possible.

If the letter is signed on behalf of some other person, write p.p.

You should never sign your name as Mr. Shri, Dr. or Col. It is ill mannerly to add such prefixes to one's signature.

INFORMAL LETTERS

It has become customary these days to send messages on birthdays, anniversaries or such other occasions through printed greeting cards. But such cards always sound impersonal and commonplace. It is like asking somebody else to convey your personal feelings. It is therefore, always better to write such a letter yourself, preferably in your own hand. Never forget to make your letter as interesting as possible.

Given below is a birthday letter:

39 Patel Road
Nagpur

14 May, 2004

My dear Ghanshyam

Let me first wish you many happy returns of the day. May this year bring you the best of peace, health and happiness.

It's a great pity that I couldn't be with you on your birthday, this year. Something unexpected held me back here. But I fondly remember the great time we had on your last birthday—the oval-shaped, chocolate cake, music and dancing. And, above all, the pleasure of meeting some of our old classmates—particularly, Ravi, Shankar, Shilpa and Srinivasan.

How's Podly, your little cat? I still remember how she sat on your sofa, and was busy licking away the icing of her share of the cake.

Please convey my best wishes to your parents.
Wish fond remembrances.

Yours ever,

Pratap

Do you know what Pandit Nehru's birthday gift for Indira was on her 13th birthday? It was a letter! Here is an excerpt of that letter.

Central Prison, Naini
October 26, 1930

My dear Indira,

On your birthday you have been in the habit of receiving presents and good wishes. Good wishes you will still have in full measure, but what present can I send you from Naini prison? My presents cannot be very material or solid. They can be of the mind and spirit . . . that even the high walls of prison cannot stop . . .

I have always thought that the best way to find out what is right and what is not right, what should be done and what should not be done is not by giving a sermon, but by talking and discussing and out of discussion sometimes a little bit of truth comes out.

A letter can hardly take the place of a talk; at best it is a one-sided affair. Imagine that I have made a suggestion to you for you to think over, as if we really were a having a talk . . .

I have written a very long letter to you. And yet there is so much I would like to tell you. How can a letter contain it? . . .

With all my love and good wishes.

Your loving father,
(J.L.Nehru)

Don't write such hackneyed sentences as:

Must stop now to catch the mail.
We're all doing well here, and wish you the same.
I've been thinking of writing to you for quite some time . . .
If there's anything I can do for you, don't hesitate to let me know.
I am always at your service.

Here are some phrases that may come handy to you in certain contexts:

A letter of recommendation

I hope it would be possible for you to talk to this gentleman . . .
This is to introduce to you someone who has worked as my typist . . .

A letter of apology

I regret any inconvenience I may have caused you . . .
I should apologize for the delay . . .

Letter of condolence

I felt very sad to hear the tragic news . . .
I convey you my deepest condolences on . . .

A message of congratulation

My heartiest congratulations on your winning . . .
Let me congratulate you on your promotion . . .
I felt excited to hear about . . .

Letter of complaint

I regret bringing to your notice . . .
I must tell you, even at the risk of offending you . . .
Would you, please, reconsider this case . . .

A letter of refusal

I'm sorry it will not be possible . . .
Unfortunately, I'd be out of town . . .

Letter of thanks

It was indeed very thoughtful of you to invite me . . .
Thank you very much for your warm hospitality . . .
With many thanks . . .

Letter of invitation

Do let me know if you could join me at dinner.
I'd be looking forward to your next visit.
I'd feel enormously pleased . . .

Miscellaneous

I look forward to hearing from you as early as possible.
Please remember me to Uncle David and Auntie Christine.
My best wishes to your family.
Please forgive me for the slight delay in answering your letter.
I seek your forgiveness for causing you so much trouble.

TASKS

1. *Write a letter to your friend on his first wedding anniversary.*

2. *Write a letter to a friend who has been blessed with a son.*

3. *Write a letter to a friend congratulating him on his winning a gold medal in an elocution competition.*

4. *Write a letter to a friend who has stood first in a State Public Service examination.*

5. *Write a letter of thanks to your uncle who has presented a wristwatch on your birthday.*

6. *Write a letter of thanks to your aunt who has invited you to the USA on a month's holiday.*

7. ***Write a letter of congratulation to a friend who has been selected Captain of the College hockey team.***

8. ***Write a letter of condolence to your friend on the death of his mother.***

FORMAL LETTERS: LETTERS OF COMPLAINT

To
The Postmaster
Sector 22
Chandigarh

3 March, 2004

Sir,

I regret to bring to your notice the fact that a letter I'd sent by speed-post from your post office on 22 February has not so far reached the addressee. I give below the relevant particulars:

(a) Receipt No.: 2350
(b) Addressee's name and address: Dr S. Vij, 13 Sapru Road, New Delhi–110002
(c) Counter No. 3

I shall feel grateful if you'd enquire into the matter and let me have a word at your earliest convenience.

Yours truly,
Brij Kishore
19 Lake Road
Sector 2
Chandigarh – 300 007

---

23 Clock Tower Road
Faizabad
21 January, 2004

To
The Commissioner of Municipal Corporation
Link Road
Faizabad – 920 518

Sir,
I wish to draw your attention to the dilapidated condition of street number three between

Wesley School and Water Tank in Srinagar Colony, South-West of Faizabad. This street has several pitfalls, and two manholes are without covers.

I shall feel grateful if you'd arrange to have the necessary repairs carried out as early as possible.

Thanking you,
Yours truly,
(Mrs) Syed Hussain

LETTER TO A NEWSPAPER

The Editor
The Indian Express
Bahadur Shah Zafar Marg
New Delhi – 110 002

Sir,

Through the columns of your esteemed national daily, I wish to draw the attention of the Police Commissioner to the lack of police patrolling in the Vasant Vihar Colony of South Delhi. There has been a spate of thefts in this area, and in spite of the repeated complaints by some of the residents, no action has been taken so far. Hardly any policeman is seen anywhere on the street at night.

It is hoped, therefore, that the Police Commissioner will direct the Circle Inspector of this zone to ensure effective police patrolling during day and night.

Thanking you,
Yours truly,

Abdul Karim
73 Bengali Market
New Delhi – 110 001

FORMAL LETTERS: LETTERS OF APPLICATION

APPLICATION FOR A POST

305 Station Road
Central Market
Kanpur – 300 009

29 March, 2004

To

The Registrar
Osmania University
Hyderabad – 500 007

Dear Sir,

Application for the post of Lecturer

In response to your advertisement in *The Deccan Chronicle* of 8 January, 2003, I wish to apply for the post of lecturer in English.

As regards my qualifications, I may state that I hold a Master's degree in English from the University of Allahabad, with distinction, securing 72% marks. At the degree examination of the same university, I was placed in the first division with a second rank.

I may here mention that as a post-graduate student, I was editor of the university magazine *The Explorer* to which I also contributed poems and short stories.

As a part of my other extra-curricular activities, I participated in several inter-collegiate public-speaking competitions. Last year, I played the role of Antony in 'Julius Caesar' as a member of the University Dramatic Club.

I hope you'd consider my application favourably.

Thanking you,
Yours faithfully,
Krishan Kant Dua

APPLICATION FOR LEAVE

13 R P. Road
Secunderabad

8 October, 2004

The Principal
Women's College
Koti
Hyderabad

Dear Madam,

As I had a minor road accident this morning, it will not be possible for me to attend college for two days. I shall, therefore, feel obliged if you grant me leave of absence for May 13 and 14.

Thanking you,

Yours faithfully,
Susheel Rao
(3rd Year student)

FORMAL LETTERS: BUSINESS LETTERS

All business letters should be brief, and written in a simple, direct manner.

21 Gandhi Road
Warangal

16 August, 2003

The Regional Manager
Orient Longman Pvt. Ltd.,
3-6-561 Himayat Nagar
Hyderabad 500029

Dear Sir,

I should feel grateful if you'd send me the following books by V.P.P. as early as possible:

1. *The Wings of Fire* by A.P.J. Abdul Kalam — one copy

2. *Roget's Thesaurus* (paper back) — one copy

3. *A Book of English Prose* by C.B. Coe — two copies

Thanking you,

Yours faithfully,

R.K. Sharma

LETTER OF INVITATION

37 The Mall,
Shimla

19 July, 2001

My dear Akbar,

My wife and I will be pleased if you and your wife could come to dinner at our house on Sunday, the 15th of March, at 7.30 p.m.

We are inviting a few other friends as well. We are sure you'd like to meet them.

Looking forward to seeing you,

Yours very sincerely,

Mohammed Saleem

A LETTER OF REFUSAL

19 Cart Road
Shimla

23 July, 2001

My dear Saleem,

It was indeed very gracious of you to invite my wife and myself to have dinner with you on Sunday, the 15th of March. But since we will be out of town next Sunday, we regret our inability to join you at dinner.

With regards,
Yours sincerely,
Ali Akbar

FORMAL INVITATION

Mr and Mrs Anil Biswas request the pleasure of having Mr and Mrs Prasant Sinha at dinner on Wednesday, the 17th of August at 7.30 p.m.

19 Prem Nagar
Nehru Colony
Meerut
12 August, 2002

DECLINING A FORMAL INVITATION

Mr. and Mrs. Anil Biswas deeply regret that due to another engagement they are unable to accept the gracious invitation of Mr and Mrs Anil Biswas to dinner on the 17th of August at 7.30 p.m.

23 Ring Road
15 August, 2002

A LETTER OF RECOMMENDATION

TO WHOSOEVER IT MAY CONCERN

The bearer of this note, Mr Siraj Hussain, has worked in my office as a clerk for six years. I found him a very competent and conscientious employee. Since our company has now been taken over by another organization, I feel sorry to lose him. I wish to recommend him very strongly for a clerical position in any concern.

J. Smith
Manager
Skyline Automobile Co.
Ahmedabad

LETTER, PLACING AN ORDER

21 Harding Road
Lucknow

12 February, 2001

To

The Circulation Manager,
The Sahara Time Weekly
Sector 11, C-1,
Noida – 705 274

Sir,

I enclose a cheque for a hundred and twenty rupees as one year's subscription to your weekly *The Sahara Time*. Kindly arrange to make this order effective immediately so that I may receive the March issue of your magazine.

Yours truly,
(Mrs) Sultana Ibrahim

Given below are some useful abbreviations, which have found usage in commercial correspondence:

Ref.:	reference
P.O.:	post office or postal order
p.p.:	by procuration
ms. mss.:	manuscript, manuscripts
Pvt. Ltd.:	Private Limited
i.o.u.:	I owe you
c.i.f.:	cost, insurance, freight (term used in shipping transportation)
bal.:	balance
a/c:	account
@:	at the rate of
appro.:	approval
cat.:	catalogue
B/s:	bill of sale
C.O.D.:	Cash on delivery
M.O.:	Money Order
at par.:	equal value
per.an.:	yearly, per annum
s.a.l.:	stamped, addressed envelope
Co.:	company
Corp.:	corporation

TASKS

1. ***Write an application to the Regional Director, BSNL for a new telephone connection.***

2. ***Write an application to the Supervisor of the Reservation / Cancellation section for a refund on your rail ticket, not used.***

3. ***Write an application to the Director of a company for the post of Public Relations Officer.***

4. ***Write an application to the Managing Director of a software company for the post of a computer operator.***

5. ***Write a letter to the editor of a daily newspaper complaining against the street dogs in your locality.***

6. *Write a letter to the Postmaster complaining about the receipt of a damaged book-parcel.*

7. *Write a letter to your landlord requesting him to undertake repairs of the house you've rented.*

8. *Write a letter to the Police Commissioner complaining about the noise at night in a hotel in your neighborhood.*

9. *Write a letter to the Project leader in your office asking him/her to grant you leave for a week as you have some personal problem. State the problem and write why it is necessary for you to atted it.*

10. *You have just read about the incident of match-fixing (in the game of cricket) in the newspaper. You are shocked to know this. Write a letter to the editor of the newspaper expressing your feelings and suggest what could be done to avoid such practices in the future.*

E-MAIL HELP PAGE: THE GRAMMAR OF E-MAIL

Have you ever wondered what these were **CUL8R or B4?** or such funny figures as these? :) :-) :D :-| [1] If you don't know these, it means you still haven't mastered the e-mail language!

I'm sure most of you have heard of the **e-mail** or the **electronic mail.** Perhaps many of you have been using it to correspond with your friends and relatives. As you know, the e-mail is not very different from a letter; it just reaches the destination **faster**. It could take days, months or even years sometimes for letters to reach their destination. Remember the unit on 'Prepositions of time' where you read the following:

A postcard sent by a Dutch gas company during the Second World War has finally reached its destination—after 62 years!

E-mails are sent through the computer and are hence take just seconds. You can write to your friends (informal letters) or correspond with companies (formal/business letters). Apart from letters, you can send photographs, documents, even music and computer programmes. So, isn't it a wonderful tool?

In this section, we basically focus on **the language** of e-mails. We thought it would be useful to present some **Do's** and **Don'ts** with regard to this.

DO'S

Use of shortcuts

We are aware of the fact that time comes at a premium these days. So how can we do the

1. These symbols are either called 'smileys' or 'emoticons'. The first one is smiling face, the second, a face with a nose (look at it sideways), the third is 'laughing' and the fourth is a grim face!

maximum required in the minimum time? Obviously, by using shortcuts. This is precisely what the modern e-mail language is all about: namely, the use of shortcuts.

Many have their own individual shortcuts, but here are a few that are frequently used. We list them below in alphabetical order:

A-Z OF E-MAIL LANGUAGE

A
asap: as soon as possible
affly: affectionately
afaik: as far as I know
atb: all the best

B
brb: be right back
b4: before
bbl: be back later
baq: back
btw: by the way

C
c:see
cam:camera
coll:college
cud:could
comp:computer
cu: see you
cul8r: call you later

D
dat:that
dunno:dont know
dc:disconnected
d8: date

E
ez: easy

F
fone:phone
frnd:friend
fyi: for your information

G
gtg:got to go

gr8:great
gotcha: got you
gonna:going to
gud:good

I
iyss: if you say so
imo: in my opinion

J
jlt: just like that

K
k:okay

L
lol—lots of laughter/love
lite—light
luk—luck
l8:late
l8r: later

M
msg: message
myob: mind your own business

N
n:and
ne:any
nite:night
no:know
ne1: anyone
no1: noone

O
obv.:obviously
ol:online
otoh: on the other hand

P
prob:problem
plz;please
ppl:people
pic:picture
p.o.a: plan of action
pcm: please call me

R
rmbr:remember
rt: right
rgds: regards
rucmng: are you coming

S
skool:school
sec:second
spk: speak

T
tc:take care
thnq: thank you

U
usp— unique selling point
u—you
ur—your

V

W
wat: what
wad: what
wid: with
wateva: what ever
wadels: what else
w8t: wait
wan2: want to
wassup: what's up

X
xlnt: excellent
xplain: explain

Y
y:why
yr: your

Z

NUMBERS

1: One
2: to, too, two,

2day: today
2 together: together
2 moro: tomorrow
2nite: tonight
4got: forgot
4 u: for you
gr8: great
cul8r: see you later

Basically, as you might have noticed, the vowels are dropped and the consonants are retained.

DON'TS

- First and foremost, remember that the abbreviated forms given above are to be used only when you mail your friends or relatives. i.e. in informal contexts. Do not use them in formal letters (business, letters for jobs, official correspondence)

- Business e-mail should be as **formal and correct in style** as any business correspondence. Exactly as in a formal letter, do use a salutation or a greeting with the recipient's name. **Use of abbreviations, even the common ones as asap (as soon as possible) or usp (unique selling point) are not appropriate for formal business correspondence.**

- **Don't end your business correspondence abruptly.** End your business correspond with your name, title (designation) and name of the organization (as you would do in any formal letter). The only thing which is not required is your signature!

To conclude this section, do be creative in your use of abbreviations when it comes to informal correspondence **but** have a :-| face and be formal in business letters sent from your computer.

PART 3

STUDY SKILLS

WORD POWER

Increasing Your Vocabulary

'Words. Was it their colours? He allowed them to glow, hue after hue: sunrise gold, the sunset and green of apple orchards, azure of waves, the grey-fringed fleece of clouds. No, it was not their colours; it was the pose and balance of the period itself.'

(James Joyce : *Portrait of the Artist as a Young Man*)

This is how James Joyce, one of the greatest writers of this twentieth century, describes his love of words. In fact, words are like human beings—they are kind or savage, loving or violent, revengeful or forgiving.

It is not always adequately understood that behind every form of writing lies the power of words. It is words that constitute a sentence. Only thereafter we may turn to grammar which helps us to understand the formation of a passage. For all this, you will need a wide range of words. It is, therefore, necessary that you should know all the ways to enlarge your vocabulary.

Here are a few guidelines :

Use of a Good Dictionary

You should always have on your desk a standard dictionary (Oxford or Random House Dictionary, if not Webster's Unabridged Dictionary)

In such a dictionary, you will not only see the meaning of an unfamiliar word but also its usage in a sentence. Remember there are two kinds of words : those which you know only for their meaning, and those which you have learnt to use in your own. It is obviously that it is only the second category of words that will help you in writing.

How can you learn to bring new words into your usage? Whenever you encounter a new word in the course of your reading, you should not only pause to look up its meaning from your dictionary but also write down in your scrap book at the sentence in which the word was used. But even that will not help you to really assimilate the word unless you also use it in a sentence of your own.

Take, for instance, the following :

'The Defence Counsel failed to make his argument credible because he had no evidence to substantiate it.' (*Credible*: that which can be believed. *Substantiate*: to establish by proof or proper evidence.)

Now let us try a variation on this sentence.

'He succeeded in making his speech *credible* by *substantiating* each point with concrete facts.'

Use of a Thesaurus

You may also find the use of a thesaurus, like *Roget's Thesaurus*, very helpful in increasing your vocabulary. This reference book is a remarkable companion to any form of writing—letter, essay or précis. This book comprises two parts—while the first part reads like an ordinary dictionary, giving a host of alternate of words, phrases and idioms), the second part is organized on the basis of ideas which you may like to express. For instance, if you wish to say that a certain ideal is difficult to achieve (a peak difficult to climb, etc.), you should look for the word *difficult* in the second part. Roget will then refer you to a certain numbered section in the first part. Given below are the alternate expressions (words, phrases and idioms) that will now await your choice.

We reproduce below a part of the section to stimulate your mind in expressing this idea.

Adj : formidable, exciting, impeccable, problematic, unwieldy, jaw-breaking, labrynthine.

Here are some phrases and idioms too :

a hard nut to crush, like squaring a circle, a Herculean task, a sticky wicket, more easily said than done, not made with rose water, in deep water, in a soup . . .

Translation as a Way of Enlarging One's Vocabulary

There is also another method which may help you increase your word power. Take a passage from any book, newspaper or magazine, and translate it into your own mother tongue. Then put aside both your translation and the original passage for a couple of days. After this brief interval, take up your own translation and render it into your own English, but without looking at the original passage. Now compare your own rendering into English with the original passage. You will then see how you chose words which were not quite appropriate. You may also notice that your own sentences were not as tightly structured as those in the original.

By using this method, you may act as your own instructor.

Now consider the following passage for this exercise :

'The sky was now covered with mountains of clouds of the skeletal remains of some primordial mammals, of an army of soldiers on the rout, ceaselessly, they sailed across the bridge from India to Pakistan, casting fugitive reflections on the tawny waters of the river.

Suddenly a flock of birds shot into the sky, and began to circle joyously over the maize fields on either side, as though scornful of the happenings on the earth below. Their spangled wings, poised securely against the wind, glimmered in the morning sun. Their puny belly tanks charged with some inexhaustible fuel, they flew round and round, up and down—and warbled.' (Reference pl.)

Note the meaning of any unfamiliar words you may have encountered in the above passage—e.g. skeletal, primordial, mammals, fugitive, tawny, flock, spangled, poised, puny, inexhaustible, warbled . . .

Look up the meanings of these words in your dictionary and try to use them in sentences of your own.

Now follow the method of translation as suggested above.

SYNONYMS AND ANTONYMS

SYNONYMS

Synonyms are words having *approximately* the same meaning—*approximately* because no two words can convey exactly the same meaning. Just as even a pair of twins will have some difference in resemblance or temperament.

Given below is a list of a few selected synonyms:

Amusement — change, recreation
Anger — rage, wrath
Ascend — climb, soar
Authentic — real, genuine
Autocrat — with absolute power
Avaricious — greedy
Aversion — hatred

Bias — prejudice
Blend — mingle
Bondage — slavery
Brave — valiant, bold
Brisk — quick

Cause — reason
Compel — force, press
Comprehend — grasp
Confer — grant
Confess — award
Conscious — aware
Contrary — opposite
Courteous — civil, gentle, well-mannered

Deplorable— unlikeable, regrettable
Despise — disdain, condemn
Dexterous — skilful
Dismal — sad
Dizzy — astounded, surprised
Eccentric — odd, queer
Efficient — competent, capable
Emphasize — stress
Endure — bear, tolerate

Enormous — large, immense
Eternal — forever, without end
Famous — reputed, renowned
Feeble — lacking strength
Felicity — joy, bliss
Ferocious — wild, savage
Foolish — stupid, unwise
Frailty — weakness

General — universal
Gentle — genial, gracious
Gigantic — huge
Giggle — laugh
Grave — serious
Guard — protect

Hazardous — dangerous
Hideous — ugly, hateful
Hinder — prevent
Holy — sacred

Idle — lazy
Illegal — unlawful, lawless
Impudent — insolent
Incite — provoke
Irritation — displeasure, annoyance

Jeer — sneer, make fun
Juvenile — youthful, immature

Keeper — guardian
Keepsake —— memento

Labour — work, toil
Laconic — concise, brief
Latent — hidden, not visible
Lax — careless
Learning — wisdom, scholarship
Liberal — open minded
Liberty — freedom
Loyal — true, devoted

Magnificent — grand, stately
Magnify — exaggerate
Marvel — wonder
Miserly — closefisted, stingy
Modest — humble, unassuming

Naïve — simple
Nativity — birth
Need — necessity
Noble — right principled, illustrious
Norm — standard
Novice — beginner

Obscene — vulgar, indecent
Obstacle — hindrance
Obstinate — stubborn
Obvious — evident, manifest
Occurrence — happening
Odd — queer, peculiar
Option — alternative, choice
Ostensibly — apparently, visibly

Pious — godly, pure, religious
Precise — exact
Proficient — skilful, expert
Profuse — extravagant, too much
Progeny — descendants
Project — scheme
Proprietor — owner
Proscribe — ban, banish, disallow
Prudent — wise, farsighted

Quake — tremble
Quantum — quantity, share
Quest — find, search
Quit — leave, give up
Quiver — tremble, shiver

Rare — unusual, infrequent
Relate — narrate, tell
Reserved — indrawn
Residue — what remains, remnant
Restraint — control, curb
Reverence — respect
Rude — ill-mannerly, discourteous

Savage — wild, cruel
Scold — reprove, reprimand, censure, condemn
Severe — strict
Shy — coy
Slander — talking ill
Sly — crafty, cunning
Solitary — lonely
Superfluous — irrelevant, unnecessary

Tacit — not openly, unspoken
Tedious — irksome
Tender — soft, gentle, delicate
Thrifty — dose-fisted, economical
Thrive — prosper, flourish
Timid — shy, weak
Tradition — old practice, convention
Transient — passing, transitory
Transparent — lucid, clear
Truism — common-place, hackneyed

Ubiquitous — present everywhere
Ultimate — end, final
Umbrage — offence, feel hurt
Underhand — dishonest, deceitful
Undergo — endure
Unique — peerless, unequalled, rare

Vacant — empty
Vacation — holiday
Vacillate — hesitate
Vagrant — vagabond
Vague — unclear
Vain — purposeless, arrogant
Valiant — courageous
Vanquish — defeat
Various — different
Venom — poison

Vulgar — indecent

Wane — decrease
Wax — increase
Wholesome — healthy
Winsome — charming, attractive
Withstand — resist, oppose
Wizard — magician

Workable — practicable

Yearly — annual
Yield — give, surrender, produce

Zeal — enthusiasm
Zest — relish, gusto

TASK 1

WORD SEARCH

SYNONYMS

```
L S O N H Y V T L W J N L S E U O R L O E P C N T
L M A M M E B U N L U O M F J M I R E L R O R S A
U S E O U N A R S D N B A T G N R A B E N L C H E
U M L H P M C L E T E O S N S A U S J T I H E E L
E U G H D I H H T T A A N O K D Y U R E E S V O O
R A U O M N L E D H I N L E E D D O A M I O G C N
L T I U R E M E D O Y E D C M I L M E T B A E E N
E A J E N I C R E F N A N A C R O U A A R A H S N
A R E U I N B Y R T E E O E R M H T D E L R S T E
T S T E E M A G T R F G E T E D E F M O B D A E T
T S H N M V M E H F N N M N E E T O C A N E A D N
A S M R R S U T O H N I T V A O S A S S F A A H D
E D L S S U H L B L R O I N A K E E L E E N E R J
D R T S I U S U G M A E W B R D A E D D E S M N A
H K A E E A E L S A M G F I U H L A N M S A E A P
E A E R R G S A A N R O H E S A N S E C E L H P C
M N N S W A I D I D U N G E E U R O T A T A L A P
N B A D O S W C A E A A N I T O O N E A O E B A R
I A O K U O L A S U F H A E F U R R R L S R R N U
C F L H E L E E M G M L N R N P G E E S B A N E T
L N T T A L I P E B G I N E R R M A I G S M A A S
N N I U B R M N S T U A R M E A L L E O N E E M S
E N N M F L E T O N N M E E G N B J L I O A E R E
E N U D E E N N E R N A E N B I N R M A S N D I T
A H E N D H L G S M N H M R O A E V A A E I L G E
```

GENUINE	INSOLENT	SCHEME	HESITATE
PREJUDICE	MOMENTO	TREMBLE	DEFEAT
AWARE	HUMBLE	CONTROL	HEALTHY
BLISS	STANDARD	IRKSOME	ANNUAL
DANGEROUS	VULGAR	OFFENCE	ENTHUSIASM

Look for these words in the square given above. Circle them as you find. Now write the synonyms of these words.

genuine: ______________________ scheme: ______________________

prejudice: ______________________ tremble: ______________________

aware: ______________________ control: ______________________

bliss: ______________________ irksome: ______________________

dangerous: ______________________ offence: ______________________

insolent: ______________________ hesitate: ______________________

momento: ______________________ defeat: ______________________

humble: ______________________ healthy: ______________________

standard: ______________________ annual: ______________________

vulgar: ______________________ enthusiasm: ______________________

TASK 2

Use an appropriate synonym (from the list given below) of the underlined word in each of the following sentences.

e.g. One should always be vigilant against an <u>adversary</u> because he may attack any time.

Answer: enemy/ opponent

prejudice gloomy stupendous share option exaggerate liberal illegal zest suffer
reticent empty valiant lenient wane stress risky prudent greedy yield

1. One who is avaricious can never be at peace with himself because he lacks contentment.
2. It is your bias against me that has made you so intolerant.
3. A wise person chooses his words very carefully before speaking.
4. It would be a gigantic project to link all the rivers in India.
5. Adequate emphasis has not been laid on the need for moral education in our schools and colleges.
6. I don't feel like going out in this dismal weather.
7. Climbing up that mountain can be very hazardous.
8. Tax evasion is unlawful and, therefore, liable for prosecution.
9. You are trying to magnify my weaknesses because you are biased against me.
10. I expect a much larger quantum of profit this year.
11. Being temperamentally very reserved, Kishore is a man of very few words.
12. Prakash had to undergo rigorous imprisonment for forging a will.
13. Since this is a vacant seat, you are welcome to take it.
14. Rana Pratap Singh was a brave warrior.
15. I feel that your affection for me has started to decrease.
16. Since he was under his employer's pressure, he had to surrender.
17. I offer you a choice to fight or surrender.
18. Being very generous, Hari gave a large share of his fortune to the poor.
19. Since the accused admitted his guilt, the judge took a mild view of his crime.
20. Prasad undertook to perform his new duties with great enthusiasm and commitment.

ANTONYMS

Antonyms are words having *(nouns, adjectives, etc.)* having opposite meanings. Like every coin with two sides, the front and the reverse. Life too is a jumble of opposites. We are often moved by feelings of hate and love, revenge and forgiveness, cruelty and kindness.

It is, therefore, quite useful to know the opposites of some words. They not only increase our vocabulary, but also make our expression fully (well) rounded.

Given below is a list of some antonyms which should constitute a part of your active vocabulary :

Given below is a list of a few selected antonyms :

Abstract — concrete, solid
Accept — reject
Acquit — charge, condemn
Advance — retreat
Affirm — refute, deny
Affluence — penury, poverty
Aggravate — worsen
Agree — conviaded
Allow — disallow, forbid
Alter — preserve, retain
Analysis — synthesis
Ancestor — descendant
Ancient — modern
Aristocrat — commoner
Arrive — leave, depart
Ascent — descent, slide down
Ask — answer
Assent — dissent
Asset — liability, burden
Attract — repel, reject
Awake — asleep

Barren — fertile
Beautiful — plain, repulsive, ugly
Belief — suspicious
Bold — cowardly, timid
Bonafides — malafides
Bravery — timidity
Bright — dull, unclear, dim, hazy

Centrifugal — centripetal
Cheap — expensive
Cheerful — sad, depressed, gloomy
Clean — dirty, soiled
Clever — foolish
Common — extraordinary
Compulsory — optional
Concord — discord
Confident — diffident, unsure
Covert — overt

Dark — bright
Death — birth
Debit — credit
Debtor — creditor
Deduction — induction
Deep — shallow
Deficit — surplus
Deliberate—unintentional, accidental
Democracy — autocracy
Diligent — laxy, lazy
Dwarf — giant

Efflux — influx
Egoism — altruism, selflessness
Elevation — depression
Emigrant — immigrant
Exclude — include
Exit — entrance
Expand — contract

Explicit — implicit
Exterior — interior
External — internal
Extravagant — stingy, miserly

Famous — unknown
Fast — loose, slow
Fat — thin
Fictitious — real
Float — sink
Foreign — native
Forget — remember
Fresh — stale
Friendly — antagonistic, hostile
Full — empty

Gather — scatter
General — special
Generous — small minded
Gentle — harsh
Genuine — spurious
Grave — happy
Guilty — innocent

Hasty — slowly
Hate — love
Haughty — modest
Heavy — light
Hero — villain
High — low
Hit — miss
Homogeneous — heterogeneous
Honour — shame
Hope — despair
Host — guest

Idle — occupied, busy
Imagination — reality
Import — export
Increase — decrease
Industrious — lazy
Inferior — superior
Inhale — exhale
Input — output

Joy — despair
Junior — senior
Justify — condemn

Kind — wild, cruel
Kindle — put out, extinguish
King — subject
Knowledge — ignorance

Landlord — tenant
Later — earlier
Latter — former
Lead — follow
Lend — borrow
Liberate — enslave
Loose — tight
Lose — find

Major — minor
Many — few
Masculine — feminine
Maximum — minimum
Memory — forgetfulness
Microcosm — macrocosm
Mild — harsh, severe
Miser — spendthrift
Monogamy — polygamy
Monotheism — polytheism
Monotony — diversity

Narrow — broad
Native — foreign
Natural — artificial
Nebulous — clear, lucid
Negative — positive

Odd — even
Offer — reject, refuse
Often — seldom
Omission — commission
Optimist — pessimist
Oral — written
Oriental — occidental
Original — duplicate, imitation

Permanent — transient, temporary
Permit — forbid
Philanthropy — misanthropy
Pleasure — pain
Practice — theory
Pragmatic — visionary, idealistic
Praise — censure, blame
Precede — succeed
Pride — humility
Profit — loss
Progress — regress
Progressive — retrograde
Promote — demote
Public — private

Queer — normal

Rash — discreet, careful
Rapid — slow
Recede — advance
Reluctant — willing
Remember — forget
Remit — receive
Retail — wholesale
Reward — punish
Right — left
Rigid — flexible
Ripe — raw
Rise — fall
Rough — smooth

Sacred — profane
Safe — dangerous
Saint — sinner
Servant — master
Sharp — blunt
Simple — complicated
Sink — swim
Smile — frown
Solid — liquid
Straight — curved, bent
Strange — known, familiar
Subjective — objective
Succeed — fail
Sure — uncertain
Sweet — sour, bitter
Sympathy — antipathy

Tall — short
Temporal — spiritual
Tense — relaxed
Thesis — antithesis
Thick — thin
Tight — loose
Top — bottom
Tranquil — tense, agitated
Transparent — opaque
Trivial — significant
True — false

Unite — separate
Upper — lower
Urban — rural
Urbane — uncultured

Vacant — occupied
Vague — definite, clear
Variable — constant
Vanguard — rearguard
Vertical — horizontal
Victory — defeat
Virtue — vice

Wake — sleep
Wide — narrow
Win — lose
Wise — stupid, foolish

Zenith — nadir

TASK 3

Provide a suitable antonym from the list given below for each of the underlined words.

e.g. My friend's speech was very abstract because he did not offer any ——— facts in support of his argument.

Answer: concrete

optional	oral	extinguishes	upper	implicit	inhale	guilty	rural	retail	repel
fertile	vice	spiritual	lazy	negative	profane	follow	exports	spurious	commission

1. She didn't feel attracted towards him; on the contrary, he ——— her.
2. The farmer saw before him a stretch of barren fields without a piece of ——— land.
3. While English is a compulsory subject in this course, you may choose any two ——— subjects: Hindi or Urdu.
4. It is always the diligent person who wins the prize, not the ——— one.
5. This poem states the central theme in a very explicit manner because it doesn't carry any ——— layers of meaning.
6. Please give me a genuine drug, not this ——— one.
7. Law holds a person innocent till he is proved to be ———.
8. Pranayam is a yogic exercise that trains a person to exhale and ——— air properly.
9. While kerosene kindles fire, water ——— it.
10. There are some who are born to lead, while others ——— them.
11. Unless you are willing to renounce all material pursuits, you cannot attain ——— peace.
12. While things are much cheaper in a wholesale market, one has to pay higher prices in a ——— shop.
13. While the path of virtue leads one to peace, —— drags one downhill to pain and misery.
14. Senior citizens are entitled to a lower berth in this train, while the ——— berth may be allotted to a younger man.
15. This novel is a mix of both sacred and ——— elements.
16. Our government should pay equal attention to the needs of both the urban and the ——— people.
17. My uncle is a famous businessman. While he imports silk from China and sells them here, he ——— readymade garments from here to the USA.
18. Please forgive me for all my errors of omission and ———.

19. While a man with a <u>positive</u> view of life is always cheerful, a person with a ——— attitude often remains depressed and worried.

20. I insist on a <u>written</u> contract as an ——— understanding will not hold water in a court of law.

TASK 4

Here are 20 words. The antonyms of these words are hidden in the square below. Look for them horizontally, vertically or diagonally.

sacred	precede	transparent	native	host
liberate	zenith	justify	remit	monotony
egoism	asset	bravery	friendly	affluence
confident	gather	deficit	accept	omission

E F T C M E O H Y P C N T E N S R I R C F N U S V
T B C I C E N V S E G S Y R P E C S S E T S C A C
C E N Y I C E I E A C T S R C D U I E I J A D O A
C I R T E F B V T E T I L E I R H E M P T E M E S
O T T U C U A R C N O A I F P A T I U T V M C I S
U E T A S L Y C E I E V F L I I D O E Q I A Y T P
E F I L S T E E O Y E I U O O I O R E S A E E T I
A P N N R G A P T Y D S N D T F P I S I A P T Y G
R I E E I T E I R E F N R Y Q S S I Y S I O O E I
Y D V T E E S E N O T D R R R V O E O R I I N D C
V O S E I R M T T S F I R I R N T V R E C L N C T
P C R U E D L L J S N A S N N Q P E E I T I C T O
V E O V C E R E F D H S N E D A I I S E T U I V E
A U I N D C I E S H S I T E L A E U V T M I E S L
D D N Y D C E D S V O I A E C F R L S R I M P Y N
I Y L T Q E M E E I S F E R P E L T I T F S T S P
S O R Y N S M T D O E O O S I I Y E Q T S D S N R
E N D H T R S N D L N P E R T E S T S S S E F A S
A S E F T P M I L D C R E O E N L T I S R O U D C
I A S D C V T T T S O I T E A I G I S L N R H G E
R Q F E C T V T O U N N T D S L G L O E I E I I L
D T E E E N E L E E D F I I T U N N O S U B S M I
P D E D I I R L E G N R E E R N N N F A F L A S I
M E D S E V A N V E L I I F S D S F F E L I F I C
F N E N O A O E T T S C A Y R C E R S S E E T S L

FORMING WORDS

USING PREFIXES

You may also increase your vocabulary by using prefixes. A prefix (*pre* – before / fix – place) is a syllable, or syllables, placed in front of a word to signify its meaning and create a new word. Many prefixes in the English language have been taken from such European languages as Greek and Latin. Some of these may have also been borrowed from Old English.

Given below is a list of a few selected prefixes which are commonly used. Try to use them in sentences of your own. Remember that the best way to learn a new word is to bring it into your own usage.

A (on) : Aglow, apart, ashore, aside, away.

Ambi (on both sides) : ambiguous, ambivalent.

Ante (before) : Antecedent, antedate, antechamber

Anti (against, opposite) : Anti-national, anti-American, anti-social, anti-secular.

Arch (chief, main) : Arch-rival, arch-angel, arch-hypocrite.

Auto (self) : Autocrat, autograph, automatic.

Bene (well) : Benefit, benevolent

Bi (two, twice) : Bigamy, bilateral, bimonthly, biennial.

Circum (around) : Circumnavigation, circumventor, circumscribe, circumference.

Co (with) : Co-ordinate, co-exist, co-operate.

Contra, counter (against) : Contraband, contravene, counteract, counter-attack, counter-statement.

De (down) : Defame, demote, desensitize, dethrone, decapitate.

Dis (apart) : Disorganize, discord, discomfort,

En, Em : Enable, encode, enrage, enlarge, endanger, embolden, embark.

Equi (equally) : Equidistant, equivocal, equivalent, equipoise, equilibrium.

Ex (out of) : Exhale, extract, extinguish, extricate, ex-Vice Chancellor.

Extra (beyond) : Extra-territorial, extraordinary, extra-terrestrial, extravagant.

Hyper (over) : Hypersensitive, hypertension, hyperbolic.

In, Ir, Im (not) : Incorrect, indecent, impossible, impassable, invisible, incurable, illegal, illegible, illogical, irregular, immaterial, irresponsible, impracticable, improper, irrational, irresistible, irreplaceable.

Inter (between) : Intercollegiate, inter-caste, international, inter-religious.

Mal, etc. (ill, evil) : Malpractice, malnutrition, malicious, maltreat, malevolent,

Mis (ill) : Misrule, misappropriate, mismanage, misplace, mistrust, mishap

Mono (single) : Monosyllable, monologue, monogamy, monotheism.

Non (not) : Nonsense, non-violent, nonentity.

Omni (all) : Omniscient, omnipresent.

Over (too much) : Overpowerful, overjoyed, overpampered

Pan : Pan-Islamic, Pan-American.

Poly (many) : Polysyllabic, polygamy, polytheism.

Post (after) : Post-script, post-war, post-mortem, post-dated.

Pre (before) : Premature, precaution, prehistoric, pre-war, pre-marriage.

Pro (for) : Pro-Chancellor, pro-secular, pro-western.

Pseudo (false) : Pseudo-secular, pseudonym, pseudo-spiritual

Re (again) : Refund, revive, re-inventing, recuperate, retract, research.

Semi (half) : Semi-final, semicolon, semi-official.

Sub (under): Sub-plot, subordinate, subconscious, sub-standard, subjugate, sub-load,

super, Sur (over) : Supernatural, supra-rational, superhuman, supervise, surpass, surplus, surcharge, survive.

Trans (across) : Transcribe, trans-pacific, transcendental, translate.

Tri (three) : Triangle, tricolour, triparticle, tricycle.

Un (not) : Unnatural, unbending, unbalanced, unattached, unable.

Un (back, against) : Unravel, unbind, unearth, uncover, unpopular.

Vice (in place of) : Vice-Admiral, Vice-President, Vice-Principal,

USING SUFFIXES

Like prefixes, words can also be formed by using a suffix. A suffix is a syllable, or syllables, placed towards the end of a word to form a new word.

We may classify these suffixes under different categories.

Formation of Concrete Nouns that represent Persons, Agents, etc.

-ard : Drunkard, niggard, dullard

-ate, -ey, -y, etc. : Advocate, jury, attorney, consignee, absentee, magnate, examinee, payee, addressee.

-er, -ier, -ary, etc. : Writer, speaker, leader, beggar, sailor, mountaineer, councillor, secretary, pamphleteer, financier luminary, mercenary, dignitary.

-ain, -on, -en, etc : Villain, captain, chieftain, librarian, pagan, citizen, warden.

-ist, -ast : Novelist, chemist, dentist, scientist, propagandist.

-ster : Songster, trickster, spinster, barrister, youngster.

-monger: Rumour-monger, iron-monger, ash-monger, scandal-monger.

Formation of Abstract Nouns that represent Condition, Quality, etc.

-age: Leverage, suffrage, foliage, bondage, percentage, personage, mileage.

-ance etc.: Attendance, brilliance, innocence, observance, sustenance.

-cy: Aristocracy, bureaucracy, democracy, lunacy.

-dom: Wisdom, kingdom, fiefdom, martyrdom, boredom, freedom.

-hood: Manhood, childhood, neighbourhood.

-ing: Singing, writing, jumping, speaking, snoring (linked to verbs)

-ion: Examination, operation, action, oration, retaliation, tension, suspension.

-ice: Service, avarice, practice, cowardice.

-ism: Capitalism, socialism, patriotism, linguism, parochialism, journalism.

-ment: Endorsement, puzzlement, enchantment, punishment, amendment.

-mony: Matrimony, harmony, ceremony, alimony.

-less: friendless, penniless, houseless.

-ness: Darkness, calmness, openness.

-red: Kindred, hatred.

-ship: Lectureship, lordship, relationship, hardship, friendship.

-th: Wealth, stealth, width, depth, health, death, birth, girth.

-tude: Altitude, longitude, fortitude, magnitude, servitude.

-ty: Cruelty, dignity, priority, loyalty, senility.

-ure, etc: Agriculture, culture, stature, grandeur, horticulture, superstructure.

Suffixes (with Verbs)

-ate: Cogitate, violate, nominate, subjugate, designate, propagate, invite, inate.

-en: Widen, brighten, lighten, weaken, sudden, gladden.

-fy: Solidify, pacify, testify, simplify, qualify.

TASK 1

Change the following adjectives into verbs : (e.g. fertile – fertilize).

national, regular, equal, clear, popular, vivid, glorious, liberal, individual, memorable, eternal, simple, internal, external, universal.

Miscellaneous

-ade: Cascade, cavalcade, brigade, blockade.

-al: Arrival, proposal, denial, capital, annual.

-ant: Discordant, proponent, descendant, tenant, merchant.

-ary: Dispensary, nunnery, dowry, pantry, cemetery, salary, monastry.

-ic ,-ique: Psychic, logic, paralytic, physique, critic, semitic.

TASK 2

Frame Abstract Nouns from the following:

Provident, secret, foolish, idiot, brave, depart, cooperate, coward, autocratic, socialist, agree, frank, jealous, high, hate, deep, young, false, prior, grand.

TASK 3

Frame Concrete Nouns from the following words:

Dull, absent, examine, absent, run, sleep, watch, sell, drive, close, invest, buy.

TASK 4

Give single words for the following:

1. One who writes novels.
2. One who keeps watch at night.
3. One who follows an art.
4. A divorced woman.
5. One who cheats others.
6. One who plays on the drum.
7. One who sells grocery.
8. One who talks too much.
9. One who flies a plane.
10. One who can read a palm.

Formation of Diminutives

(dimunitive – *is small, little, tiny*

e.g. *rivulet is a reduction of river, a tiny stream*)

-let: Rivulet, booklet, streamlet, owlet.

-ling: Stripling, weakling, yearling, duckling.

-en: Maiden, kitten, chicken.

-et: Kitchenette, cigarette, packet, coronet.

-y: Puppy, birdie

Adjective Suffixes

-al: International, national, provincial, loyal.

-ar: Secular, circular, lunar, solar, perpendicular.

-ary: Contrary, honorary, arbitrary, necessary.

-ant, Magnificient, brilliant, obedient, subservient, variant.

-able, Capable, salable, lovable, visible, audible, likable, potable.

-ed: Bearded, turbaned, moneyed, divorced.

-en: Earthen, brazen, golden, sodden.

-esque: Grotosque, statuesque, picturesque.

-ful: Fearful, tearful, willful, hopeful, cupful, brimful.

-ic: Public, plastic, aquatic, patriotic, telegraphic, antique, telepathic, unique.

-ine: Feminine, masculine, divine, saline, Swadesh, British, rubbish, thievish, reddish, greenish, bluish, boorish, amateurish, lavish.

-ive: Possessive, retrogressive, massive, active, missive, talkative, possessive, deceptive.

-lent: Turbulent, circumvent, violent, virulent.

-less: Meaningless, penniless, fearless, lawless, jobless.

-ly (like): Savagely, friendly, womanly, manly, cowardly, kindly, graciously.

-ory: Introductory, contradictory, valedictory.

-ous: Furious, curious, luxurious, dangerous, valorous, murderous.

-some: Meddlesome, handsome, fulsome, wearisome, quarrelsome, wholesome.

-ward: Forward, backward, eastward.

TASK 5

Frame Adjectives from the following:

a. literature, spirit, circle, triangle, sun, earth, pity, picture, wood, gold, sound, slave, boor, progress, violence, radiance, glory, preface, filth, friend.

b. Prevail, resolve, move, see, forbid, learn, drink, include, deceive, abuse, possess, melt, shrink, hide, curve, defeat, mark, signify, collect, hurt, marry, sleep.

WORDS OFTEN CONFUSED

Affect: (to influence, feign or to pretend) The icy wind affected his lungs. The +student affected headache to leave his class.
Effect : (to bring about) The assembly effected many changes in the act.

Accelerate: (to increase) The policeman accelerated his motor bike to catch the thief.
Expedite: (to hasten) All measures were taken to expedite the construction of the bridge.

Ancient: (very old) Many people still cling to ancient customs and traditions.
Antique: (belongings to the past) Many antique idols in the temple have been stolen.

Apprehend: (to grasp, catch) The thief was apprehended before he could escape.
Comprehend: (to understand) Since his speech was very abstract, very few people could comprehend it.

Assent: (agreement) Both parties cancelled the agreement by mutual assent.
Ascent: (climbing up) The ascent to that hill-top is a very difficult task.

Amiable: (likeable) If Ram Kishore is very popular it is because of his amiable qualities.
Amicable: (friendly) At some stage both India and Pakistan will have to arrive at an amicable solution over all disputes.

Adapt: (make something suitable) When you live in a foreign country, you should adapt yourself to its customs.
Adopt: (to take someone into a new relationship) Since Ram Pratap had no children of her own he has adopted his nephew as his son.

Apposite: (suitable) He supported his statement with apposite examples.
Opposite: (contrary) Antonyms are words opposite meanings.

Allusion: (reference) This poem has many allusions to British history.
Illusion: (false) Don't be under this illusion that your brother will help you in the crisis.

Abstract: (a short summary) His secretary gave him an abstract of the case in just a page.
Extract: (a passage taken from any chapter, book, etc.) This is just an extract from *The Bhagvad Gita*.

Affection: (love) Vinod has great affection for his elder sister.
Affectation: (outward show or artificiality) Affection in a person's behaviour will make him unpopular.

Artful: (shrewd, cunning) Being artful, Khan do not brusted by anyone.
Artificial: (not natural) Artificial flowers have colour but no smell.

Artist: (anyone who practices some fine art – e.g. painting) Picasso was the greatest artist of the twentieth century.
Artisan: (one who practices any useful crafts) Artisans like weavers or black smith should be respected as useful members of our society.

Collision: (rash contact) This morning there was a collision between a truck and a scooter.
Collusion: (secret, some illegal purpose) There was a collusion between the policeman and the criminal.

Compliment: (regards) I am sending you the book with the compliments of the author.
Complement: (anything that completes) Identify the complement of the subject in this sentence.

Confident: (certain) He was confident of winning the prize.
Confidential: (secret) Since this is a confidential letter its contents should not be revealed to any one.

Comprehensive: (full) this is not comprehensive because it does not cover all the details.
Comprehensible: (understandable) This poem is not comprehensible.

Confirm: (endorse) I wish to confirm my arrival tomorrow.
Conform: (comply with) Your actions does not conform my directions.

Contagious: (to spread by contact) Flu is a contagious disease.
Contiguous: (side by side) the open land contiguous to his farm has led to a legal dispute.

Destiny: (fate) It is not destiny but our action that condition our future.
Destination: (goal) My ultimate destination in life is to become a national leader.

Dual: (double) This word has a dual meaning.

Duel: (a fight between two adversaries) When two criminals of the same gang fell out, they fought a duel with swords.

Disease: (illness) Cancer is a fatal disease.
Decease: (death) After his uncle's decease, he inherited all his property.

Eligible: (qualified) Since he is underage, he is not eligible for the post of constable.
Illegible: (not readable) Your hand-writing is illegible. Please send me a typed letter.

Emigrate: (to go out one's country to settle abroad) Several Chinese have emigrated to the USA in the last few years.
Immigrate: (to take residence in not one's own) United Arab Emirates is now controlling the immigration of Indian labourers into Dubai.

Eminent: (famous) V.S. Naipaul is an eminent writer.
Imminent: (likely to just happen) Another earthquake is imminent in Indonesia.

Facilitate: (make easy) America has offered to facilitate the dialogue between India and Pakistan
Felicitate: (congratulate) A function was organized to felicitate on his winning Padma Shree.

Imaginary: (not real) The hero in this novel is a purely imaginative character.
Imaginative: (endowed with imagination) Tagore was a very imaginative poet, novelist and story-writer.

Industrial: (pertaining to industry) Japan is one of the most leading industrial countries in the world.
Industrious : (hard-working) Shyam is a very industrious student.

Ingenuous: (open) Mumtaz is a woman of very ingenuous temperament.
Ingenious: (clever) He is very ingenious because he can find new ways to do everything.

Judicial: (legal) Every advocate is also a judicial officer.
Judicious: (far sighted) He is very judicious in his choice of friends.

Momentary: (temporary) All earthly pleasures are momentary.
Momentous: (very significant) Mahatma Gandhi took a momentous decision to launch his Quit India movement against the British rulers.

Metal: (like gold, iron, etc.) Gold is the precious metal.
Mettle: (spirit, courage) He proved his mettle as a tough bargainer.

Official: (pertaining to an office) This is an official letter, not a private letter.
Officious: (offering service that is not wanted)

Popular: (liked by everyone) President Abdul Kalam is very popular with children.
Populous: (heavily populated) China is the most populous co9untry in the world.

Principal: (top man) Tea is the principal export from Assam. Dr. Das is the Principal of Badruka College.
Principle: (general rule) We should follow the principle of truth and non-violence.

Reverend: (deserving respect) the Acharya was a reverend old saintly man dressed with saffron clothes.
Reverent: (feeling reverence) They entered the temple in a reverent frame of mind.

Stationary: (not moving) There are some stationary stars in the sky.
Stationery: (writing materials) I have to buy some stationery for my son who is studying at the Jesus Mary School.

Verbal: (belonging to words) This is only a verbal statement. I want everything in writing.
Verbose: (wordy) He is very verbose because he can talk for hours together without meaning anything.

WORDS FOLLOWED BY APPROPRIATE PREPOSITIONS

Abide by : You must *abide by* the rules of this game.

Abound in : This tank *abounds* (holds plenty of) in fish.

Abounds with : The jungles of Madhya Pradesh *abound with* dacoits.

Absent from: The clerk has been *absent from* duty for a whole week.

Absorbed in : Kamala is fully *absorbed in* her painting.

Abstain from : The drivers *abstained from* duty yesterday.

Accede to : The principal didn't *accede to* the student's request.

Access to : He has no *access to* the Home Minister.

Acquainted with : I am not *acquainted with* the Commissioner of Police.

Acquitted of : Ram was *acquitted of* the charge of copying in the examination.

Addicted to : Saleem is *addicted to* gambling.

Adjacent to : The post office is *adjacent to* his house.

Admit to : His mother was *admitted to* the Apollo Hospital.

Affiliate to : The school is *affiliated to* the Board of Secondary Education.

Agree to : I cannot *agree to* your proposal.

Agree with : They Chinese food does not *agree with* me.

Agree upon : They *agreed upon* a uniform plan of action.

Aim at : I cannot *aim at* winning the prize.

Alight from : I was the first to *alight from* the train.

Allotted to : This task has been *allotted to* me.

Allude to : He *alluded to* a passage in the Bhagvad Gita.

Amazed at : I am *amazed at* your forgetfulness.

Anxious to : He is very *anxious to* meet his cousin in Delhi.

Anxious about : He was *anxious about* his mother's health.

Apologise to : The student was ordered to *apologise to* his teacher for his behaviour.

Appeal to : They have now *appealed to* the Supreme Court.

Aptitude for : Kishore has an *aptitude for* music.

Arrive at : We have *arrived at* station very late.

Avail ... of : I will *avail* myself of the next opportunity to apply for the post.

Aware of : I was not *aware of* his evil design.

Bank on : You should not *bank on* his help.

Bargain for : He *bargain for* a better price for the camera.

Bear with : We had to *bear with* our neighbour playing loud music at night.

Believe in : I don't *believe in* his promises.

Beneficial to : Deep breathing is very *beneficial to* health.

Bent on : My own brother seems to be *bent on* harming me.

Beware of : *Beware of* talking to strangers in a bank.

Boast of : He *boasts of* her father's high position.

Blind to : Every father is *blind to* his son's failings.

Break into : The thief *broke into* the house at midnight.

Bring about : He has *brought about* many reforms.

Bring up : All parents should *bring up* their children with great care.

Brood over : Don't brood over your failure in the examination.

Call at : I may *call at* my uncle's house on my way back from college.

Call for : The teacher has called for his explanation for being late in class.

Care for : I do *care for* my friends.

Care of : We should take *care of* our parents in their old age.

Charge with : He is charged with the murder of his neighbour.

Close to : His shop is close to my house.

Close by : the grocery store is close by.

Come across : On our way to the museum we cam across several tourists.

Commend to : Will you please commend to your employer.

Comment on : Please comment freely on the story I have written.

Compete with : Both Aloke and Rana are competing with each other for the top position in class.

Complain of : He has been complaining of headache since morning.

Complain against : I have complained against the rude behaviour of a traffic constable.

Comply with : He has been ordeed to comply with the directions.

Confer on : The Padma Bhushan was conferred on Jagjit singh, the ghazal singer.

Confide in : Can I confide in you in this matter?

Confident of : He is very confident of winning the prize.

Confine to : I have been confined to my bed for a bone fracture.

Congratulate on : He congratulated me on my success in the IAS examination.

Conscious of : It is better to be conscious of one's limitation.

Contrary to : You have acted to our expectations, contrary to my advice.

Conversant with : I am not conversant with the rules of this game.

Convict of : He is convicted of forgery and is liable to be jailed.

Craving for : Sham has a craving for horse-racing.

Cure of : I am cured of my back pain by this yogic exercise.

Deal in : My brother deals in stationery.

Decide upon : I have decided upon a strategy to win the contract.

Deficient in : Fast food is deficient in nutrition.

Deal with : I know how to deal with those who are rude to me.

Depend on : Those who depend on others always come to grief.

Deprive of : He was deprived of his property by his own brother.

Derive from : His income is mainly derived from his royalties.

Desirous of : I am desirous of studying abroad.

Deviate from : One should never deviate from the principles of honest living.

Diffident about : I feel diffident about winning this boxing match.

Disagree with : He disagreed with me on several occasions.

Disgrace to : He is a disgrace to his school.

Dispose of : I have decided to dispose of my old typewriter.

Dissuade from : I have failed to dissuade him from investing in stocks and shares.

Disgusted with : I am disgusted with my brother's lying.

Distinct from : This plan is distinct from the plan I had tune, but quite distinct proposed earlier.

Distinguish between : We should learn to distinguish between a true and false friend.

Due to : The delay in replying to your letter was due to my sickness.

Dwell on : The speaker dwelt at great length on the problem of corruption in our society.

Eligible for : Geeta is not eligible for appointment as accountant.

Engaged on : He is presently engaged on a new project.

Enticed into : He was enticed into drug trafficking for quick money.

Entrusted with : He was entrusted with the responsibility of finding a suitable match for his cousin.

Envious of : I am very envious of your success as a sales executive.

Equal to : He equal to any task assigned to him.

Excuse for : You have no excuse for losing your temper.

Exchange for : He wants to exchange his old house for a new apartment.

Familiar with : He is not quite familiar with the customs of this community.

Fancy to : I have taken a fancy to watching birds.

Fascination for : I have a fascination for antique.

Fond of : He is very fond of strawberries.

Forgetful of : He is forgetful of his responsibilities.

Furnish with : I want to be furnished with some information before I can take any decision in the matter.

Get at : He want to get at the bottom of the case.

Get over : You should try to get over your depression.

Gifted with : Rani is gifted with a talent for drawing cartoons.

Guard against: You must guard against those who indulge in back biting.

Guilty of : I am not guilty of any wrong doing.

Hand over : I have already handed over my charge as Principal of the college.

Hanker after : Those who hanker after publicity are never at peace with themselves.

Heir to : Prince Charles is heirs to the throne of England.

Hit upon : I hit upon an idea to start a new business.

Identical with : I don't wish to be identified with these strikers.

Identity of : The identity of the suicide bomber is still not fully established.

Ignorant of : I am ignorant of his background.

Included in : He has not been included in the team.

Indebted to : I am indebted to my parents for their financial support.

Indignant at : He was indignant at the misconduct of her own brother.

Inquire into : A Commission was appointed to inquire into the cause of the communal riots.

Inquire after : I inquired after his health from his neighbours.

Insist on : He insisted on my explanation for not attending the meeting.

Interfere in : You should not interfere in my private affairs.

Invited to : I have not been invited to the wedding.

Jealous of : Don't be jealous of winning the prize.

Join in : I joined (with) them in celebrating Diwali.

Jump to : He jumped to the conclusion without knowing all the facts.

Keen on : I am very keen on going abroad for further studies.

Keep up : Keep up your spirits even in hard times.

Last for : These provisions will not last even for a week.

Lead to : This may lead to serious consequences subsequently.

Limit to : There is a limit to my patience.

Look up to : I look up to my teachers for advice.

Look after : We must look after our parents in their old age.

Lost to : He is lost to all notions of good behaviour.

Lost in : He is always lost in his fantasies.

Manage with : I cannot manage with just a couple of hundred rupees per week.

Match for : He is no match for Ghulam Ali.

Meddle with : Never try to meddle with other people's affairs.

Meet with : Lata met with a scooter accident.

Mix with : Don't mix with undesirable.

Moved by : He was greatly moved by his friend's message of condolence.

Name after : this road was named after Sardar Patel.

Negligent in : Pandey has been very negligent in his duties.

Object to : I strongly object to your accusations against me.

Obliged to : I am obliged to my uncle for his support in this matter.

Occur to : It occurred to me that I had not thanked him adequately enough.

Officiate for : I have been officiating for the Principal for about a year.

Opposed to : I am opposed to the idea of moving to another town.

Originate in : The row originated in a minor altercation.

Overwhelmed with : I was overwhelmed with his generous help.

Part with : He was compelled to part with his stereo system to clear his loan.

Part from : He parted from his old classmates very sadly.

Partial to : He is not partial to anyone in this matter.

Passion for : I have a passion for stamp collecting.

Pass for : He tried to pass for a policeman to cheat the villager.

Popular with : This teacher is very popular with his students.

Prefer to : I'd prefer to resign rather than suffer indignities.

Prejudice against : He is prejudiced against members of the community.

Preside over : The Governor presided over the inaugural function.

Prevent from : He was prevented from entering the city for a month.

Pride in : I take pride in my father's achievements.

Proficient in : He is very proficient in public speaking.

Protest against : He protested against his dismissal.

Puzzled at : I am puzzled at his attitude.

Qualified for : Sundip is not qualified for the post of lecturer in English.

Quarrel over : Why quarrel over trivial matters?

Ready for : He is ready for any assignment given to him.

Reconciled to : I am now reconciled to living in this old house.

Reconciled with : He is now reconciled with his wife.

Recover from : I have still not recovered from the shock of his betrayal.

Refer to : Let me refer to my previous letter to know what I had said in this matter.

Refrain from : He must refrain from making wild allegations against me.

Regard for : He have great regard for me.

Relations with : His relations with me gone bitter.

Rely on : I can't rely on you in this case.

Remarkable for : This engine is remarkable for its strength and efficiency.

Repent of : I am willing to repent of the harsh words I have spoken against you.

Reputation for : Kanta Rao has a reputation for letting down his friends.

Retired from : I retired from service ten years ago.

Revenge on : He took revenge on his enemies.

Room for : There is room for any misunderstanding in this matter.

Run down : He has always tried to run down even though I have never said a word against him.

Run out of : My car has run out of petrol.

Search for : They are busy searching for the missing tourists.

Sensitive to : She is very sensitive to any unkind remark about her.

Short of : They are short of labourers.

Sick of : I am sick of his lame excuses.

Similar to : Their hotel is similar to the one I stayed at last time.

Steeped in : He is steeped in old rituals.

Stoop to : He stooped to mean tactics.

Submit to : I cannot submit to your unreasonable demands.

Subscribe to : I cannot subscribe to such old beliefs.

Suitable for : This house is suitable for you.

Sure for : He is sure of winning the match.

Suspected of : He is suspected of harbouring the criminal.

Suspicious of : Why are you suspicious of my motive.

Tamper with : He is likely tampered with the evidence.

Testify to : He can testify to my integrity.

Thankful for : He was thankful to me for my recommendation.

Tired of : she is tired of asking her father to send her abroad.

Touch upon : I will touch upon this issue in the course of my speech.

Trifle with : I cannot let him trifle with my emotions.

True to : He is always true to his word.

Understanding with : He has an understanding with his business partner.

Used to : Most educational institutions are used to periodic strikes these days.

Useful for : These instructions are useful for succeeding in your career.

Versed in : He is well-versed in classical music.

Victim of : I have been a victim of this betrayal.

Wanting in : Ashok is wanting in compassion and trust.

Worthy of : I shall try to be worthy of your trust.

Yield to : I cannot yield to his pressure.

Zealous for : He is a zealous social reformer.

Zest for : I have a zest for jogging.

PRÉCIS WRITING

Read the following passage.

> I thank you for inviting me to inaugurate the seminar on social justice, a subject that is very close to my heart.
>
> We should remember today Mahatma Gandhi who awoke our nation to the imperative need for social equality and rescue underprivileged sections of our society from the indignity of neglect and injustice. My heart bleeds when I visualize the appalling conditions of the so called untouchables who live in our villages and towns. Didn't Mahatma Gandhi always remind us that India would never savour true independence till we discard amidst ourselves all barriers of caste, creed and colour. In the eyes of God, all His creators are the same.
>
> It is a pity that social justice has so far remained with us as only an empty slogan that we hear mostly at the time of national elections. That is the time when our politicians talk about the upliftment of the weaker sections of our society. Once the elections are over, all such slogans lie buried under a thick layer of dust. To Mahatma Gandhi alone was social justice his only gospel of truth. No wonder, Einstein who lived at the same time as Gandhi remarked about him that for generations to come, people will hardly believe that such a man as Gandhi walked about the face of the earth in flesh and blood.

I'm sure you do have such passages in your prose text or in any other textbook which you need to read and remember from the examination point of view. How do you do it? It is necessary to shorten the passage and remember the gist or the main points.

If you were to shorten the passage and just mention a gist of it, what would you do? Here are some steps that you could follow:

- As you read this passage, you may see that it is a speech delivered by a social reformer on the subject of "Social Justice". So this is obviously the title which is repeated not only in the very outset but also in the opening sentence of the second paragraph.
- There is also some repetition in this speech, and the speaker has used rhetoric and metaphor. ('My heart bleeds ...' 'the slogan lies buried under a think layer of dust.'). Try to ignore these and concentrate on the central points.
- Make a note of the main points.

Main points

1. This is an inaugural speech on social justice.

2. The speaker invokes Mahatma Gandhi's ideas for social justice.

3. How the underprivileged members of our society have remained neglected.

4. No national progress will be possible unless all differences in our society are removed.

5. How politicians exploit these poor people, feeding them on promises which they never kept after elections.

6. To Mahatma Gandhi alone was social justice a matter of faith.

7. The speaker refers to Einstein's tribute to Gandhi.

Here is a summary or a 'précis' of the passage.

Social Justice

In his inaugural address to the seminar on social justice, the speaker reminds his countrymen to rededicate themselves to the ideals of social equality. He feels that no real national development could be possible without the active participation of these socially handicapped people, which could be achieved only when the based of discrimination based on religions and social is eradicated.

He feels distressed to see how these people are fed on false promises at the time of national elections but never honoured in deed.

Précis (A french word pronounced praycee) means summary, abridgement—shortening of a passage (written or spoken statement) to a smaller length.

In our age of high speed, our administrators and politicians have hardly any time to look through a long document. They would, therefore, prefer to have it abstracted to a readable size, usually one third of the original length, unless otherwise specified. This has made précis-writing acquire a special significance today.

Here are a few guidelines for such an exercise.

- It is advised that a student should first read the passage just to understand what it is all about. What is the writer trying to say? At the preliminary stage, it should be enough to understand the main gist of the passage. Nothing more.

- It is now time to read the passage again, this time very closely. Now try to get down the essential points on a separate piece of paper. Don't change the order of these points unless your rearrangement of the points will bring the theme of the original passage to a clearer focus.

But, as mentioned, it is advisable not to tamper with the original order.

- As you are engaged in enumerative, the central points, you may start underlining certain sentence, words or phrases. This should be avoided because you may then feel tempted to repeat some of these sentences in your précis. Of course, you may find it necessary to use a word or two from the original passage. But even here it is better to think of using another which carries the same meaning. This is where a synonym may come heavily. For instance, if the writer refers to 'certain *cardinal* principles of evaluation . . .,' you may use the words *central* or *basic* for *cardinal*, and refer to *evaluation* as *assessment*.

- In the process of summarizing a passage, you may find it possible to substitute a single word for an entire sentence. For instance, instead of saying that 'Gandhi and Einstein lived at the same period of time,' you may just refer to Gandhi and Einstein as 'contemporaries'. We have given at the end of this chapter a brief list of some useful one-word substitutes.

- Since a précis writer is engaged in the exercise of condensing the original passage to a much shorter length he must avoid :

a. repetitions, if any, in the original statement
b. retaining similes and metaphor, if they, used by the original writer. Since they are often used to make the writing colourful and interesting, they have no place in a précis which is concerned with only the basics of a theme. In other words, a précis writer should always be prepared to throw the chaff and retain only the kernel.
c. retaining examples or illustrations which the original writer may have used to endorse his points. But there is no place in a précis for such elaborations.

- Since a précis is always written in the indirect form (reported speech), all quotations should be changed to the third person. This is because a précis writer has no voice of his own. He is only a reporter, who is required to reproduce as faithfully as possible what has been said in the original passage. For instance, consider Lokmanya Tilak's words: 'Freedom is my birthright, and I will shed the last drop of my blood to win independence for my country.' This statement will appear in the précis as: 'Lokmanya Tilak always proclaimed that freedom was his birthright, and he would shed the last drop of his blood to win independence for his country.'
- If, as explained above, a précis writer is only a reporter, he should not induct any comments of his own into his summary. It would be like a postman opening a letter and adding his own comments before handing it over to the addressee. Therefore, the merit of a good précis lies in its faithful representation of the original though in a shorter and simpler form.

- As mentioned above, a summary is ordinarily one third of the length of the original passage, unless some other limit is specified. It is, therefore, advised that you should mention at the end of your précis the number of words used in your précis. You may, how ever, exceed in limit by about five or ten words.

- The real test of a good précis is that it should read like an original piece of writing, and not a few points loosely strung together. There should be a progression in your précis, one point linked to another, and the entire précis acquiring a pattern of its own. In other words the reader of your précis should take it as a fresh piece of writing, tightly structured.

- Finally, a précis should carry a suitable title, even if it is not specifically called for. A title is like a crown placed on the head of a person. It is his mark of identity. So does the title of a passage announce its content through the title.

If you read any passage closely enough, you may see that its title is either suggested in the opening sentence or in the concluding sentence. It may also appear somewhere in the middle of a passage because most authors work towards the climax between the beginning and the conclusion of their theme.

A title should be as brief as possible. It is usually without a verb, with each word beginning with a capital letter except conjunctions and prepositions. See the following example :

The Man and his Dog.

The Heart of Darkness.

Taming of the Shrew.

The Pleasure of Reading One's Writing.

TASK 1

Summarise the following passages, supplying a suitable title in each case:

Reformers look forward to a time when efficient social organization and perfected machinery will do away with the necessity for severe and prolonged labour, making possible for all men and women a amount of leisure such as is enjoyed at the present day only by a privileged few. Nobody, in that golden age, will need to work more than four or five hours a day. The rest of every man's time will be his own, to do with whatsoever he likes.

It is difficult for any sensitive person not to sympathize with these aspirations. But sympathy with an ideal need not make the sympathizer uncritical of it; one may feel strongly, but one must not therefore cease to think. The majority of human beings are oppressed by excessive labour of the most senseless kind. That fact may, and indeed should, arouse our indignation and our pity. But these emotions must not prevent us from criticizing the project of those who wish to change the present state of things. The social reformers desire to see a dispensation under which all men will have as much, or nearly as much, leisure as is enjoyed by the leisured classes today. We may be permitted to doubt, for all our sympathy, whether the consummation is really, after all, so much to be desired.

TASK 2

Deep-rooted in man is the instinct to search for truth, an insatiable desire for knowledge and understanding. It is a noble instinct, a lofty desire. There is, however, another aspect of science. There is also in man the desire for knowledge of the laws of nature in order to press them into his service. Herein lies the origin of applied science. To increase knowledge for the sheer delight of knowing and understanding, to further the application of that knowledge in order to ease the burden of existence : these are the two main features of the twofold aspect of science. Each has its beauty and its poetry.

At all stages in the history of science a feeling for beauty has guided and directed the minds of scientists in their researches. They venture to try the explanation which to them seems intellectually the most beautiful, and the astonishing thing is that their effort often brings them success. Is there some mysterious link between truth and beauty?

Let us now turn to that aspect of science which is concerned with its application. Applied science has transformed civilization and the conditions of man's existence, and will doubtless transform them still more in the future. By its aid all the forces of nature are gradually harnessed to man's service; heat, electric light, atomic energy, all are subject to man's control. Sound and picture are flung to the four corners of the world, and the earth grows small for the speed of modern transport. The world is transformed daily by the advance of applied science and there appears to be no limit to progress.

TASK 3

This problem of the art of living is one which for two thousand years has interested and perplexed the world's philosophers . . . Most people would agree that, apart from the eternal varieties, the art of living consists in the achievement of happiness and in the avoidance of unhappiness . . .

Happiness has little to do with enjoyment or even pleasure; it is something far more reputable than self-indulgence. Happiness can only be found in the free and successful expression of one's own personality. Happiness, or the art of living, consists in the free and successful expression of one's own personality. It is far more than selfishness or self-seeking. People who are selfish or self-centered or conceited have not begun to learn the art of living; they have not mastered even the ABC of the art. Of all the miserable people in the world there are none so miserable as those who think only of themselves and whose every motive is a self-seeking motive.

Every man or woman born into this world is given certain personal virtues and cursed with certain personal defects. If he or she seeks to express his or her own personality, which I hold to be the art of living, he must strive always to express his virtues and to suppress his defects. He must not express the worst in himself; he must express the best in himself. He will never be happy if he falls into the dreary round of selfishness.

TASK 4

One of the banes of contemporary civilization is TV viewing. Not enough attention has been paid to its adverse effects on our young men who remain glued to the screen for hours together. Back from school or college, they settle down in front of the idiot box, entirely lost to the world outside. Of course, everyone needs a little relaxation after the day's grind, but to remain absorbed in serials, cartoons or sports is a different matter. There is indeed an element of truth in the maxim that all work and no play made Jack a dull boy. But it may be equally true to say that all play and no work made him unfit to face the challenges of life.

Very few of our young men are interested in the news channels, or any debates on contemporary social, moral, political or religious problems. They just switch on their TV to view some story of love, crime or sex. Consequently, many of them have taken to such crimes as stealing, liquor or drugs. It is unfortunate that most parents find it impossible to keep their children away from the TV. But it is imperative that unless our society finds a way out of this malaise, the future of our country is doomed to disaster.

PARAGRAPH WRITING

Read this paragraph from Sir William Slim's essay titled 'What is courage?'

'All men have some degree of physical courage. It's surprising how much. Courage, you know, is like having money in the bank. We start with a certain capital of courage, some large, some small, and we proceed to draw on our balance. But don't forget courage is an expendable quality. We can use it up.'

This is a paragraph taken from an essay. But although it is a part of a larger piece of writing, what strikes you as you read it, is its **distinct identity**, because, structurally speaking, a **paragraph is a self-contained unit.** This paragraph defines courage on a direct and forthright manner. You may notice that it stands as an independent unit of thought and belief.

A paragraph constitutes a unit in any form of writing—a précis, a letter or an essay. It may be a part of a page or a chapter. And yet it is complete and well-rounded in every respect.

Each paragraph usually announces its main theme in the opening sentence. But the most important thing is it should also develop it to the end so as to become a complete unit. Take, for instance, the following paragraph taken from an essay by Aldous Huxley on 'Work and Leisure.'

'To Tolstoy the whole idea of universal leisure seemed absurd and even wicked. The social reformers who held up the attainment of universal leisure as an ideal he regarded as madman. They aspired to make all men like those rich, idle, urban people among whom he had passed his youth and whom he so profoundly despised. He regarded them as conspirators against the welfare of the race.'

Tolstoy is here presented as someone who was totally against any concept of leisure. He was, it is abundantly clear, for the opposite idea: 'Work is worship'. Thus, the paragraph makes a statement of its own.

GUIDELINES FOR WRITING A PARAGRAPH

- The opening sentence in a paragraph should state the theme as incisively as possible. Note the opening sentence in the paragraphs illustrated above:
  'To Tolstoy the whole idea of universal leisure was absurd and even wicked.'
  'All men have some degree of physical courage.'

- Now develop the main idea announced in the opening sentence to make it sound clear and complete. Of course, there is never much scope in the body of a paragraph to elaborate a point fully.

- Each sentence in a paragraph should lead the reader progressively to the next sentence, like links in a chain. Or, to use another metaphor, like the bogies in a train. There should be no abrupt pause between one sentence and the other.

- Write short and simple sentences as far as possible. Remember that brevity always lends punch to an argument or a description.

- The concluding sentence in a paragraph should be like putting a lid on a kettle. It should round off the entire theme as neatly as possible. Note the last sentence in the paragraph on 'Work and Leisure':
  'He regarded them as conspirators against the welfare of the race.'

DIFFERENT CATEGORIES OF PARAGRAPHS

1. LOGIC AND REASONING

A paragraph that involves the reader in some argument with a positive or negative stance, always tries to clinch a particular point of law in one way or the other. For instance, Tolstoy is clearly for work and not leisure.

2. DESCRIPTION

A descriptive paragraph, on the other hand, is just a visual form of writing. It is like doing a miniature painting. It should hold the reader's eye with its vivid details.

3. NARRATION

A paragraph in a narrative form of writing is always designed to carry a story forward, dramatically. It functions as an organic segment of a larger piece of writing.

4. A FACTUAL STATEMENT

Such a paragraph should not attempt to take sides as it is primarily intended to present a factual statement as objectively as possible. There is no scope here for the writer's personal comments. Such a paragraph should let the facts speak for themselves.

TASK 1

Write a paragraph, of about sixty words, on each of the following subjects:

1. Television viewing is a bane of contemporary civilization (logic and reasoning)

2. Describe a street fight (descriptive)

3. A burglary in a neighbour's house (narrative)

4. Road accidents in your city (factual)

A NET DIRECTORY: SOURCES FROM THE NET

This is the age of the internet. It has indeed made our life easier, hasn't it?

There is plenty of information available in the net to improve your grammar, vocabulary, letter writing skills which could be useful for you; more generally, to help you learn correct English. The directory that we have provided below is not comprehensive, but it will do to make a beginning.

Remember that the sites given here are for teachers as well as learners of English.

Let us classify the material available under two broad headings:

- Specifically for English
- General

As our main focus is on grammar, we also mention sources from the net that are dedicated to the teaching and learning of grammar.

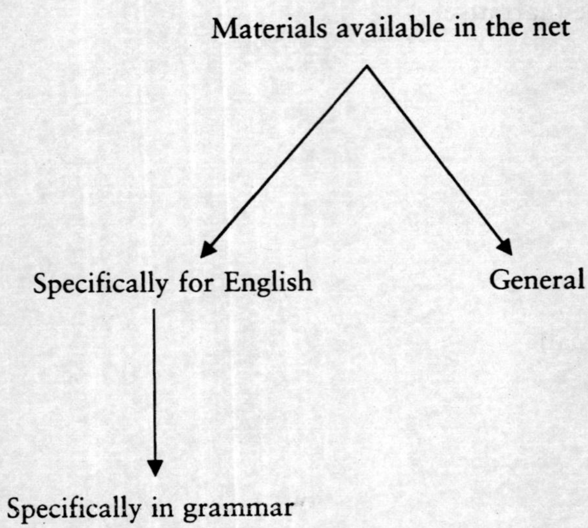

General

www.independent.co.uk
www.guardian.co.uk
www.bbcnews.com
http://education.guardian.co.uk
www.smarterkids.com
www.hut.fi/~dpihk/Library/dictiona.htm

Specifically for English

www.eslgames.com
www.eslcafe.com
www.aaaefl.co.uk
www.cant.ac.uk/depts/acad/languages/tefl_res.htm
www.learnenglish.org.uk
www.bbc.co.uk/worldservice/llearningenglish/index.shtml
www.edufind.com

Specifically for grammar

http://cctc2.commnet.edu/grammar/
http://www.wsu.edu/~brians/errors/errors.html
http://www.nckcn.com/homepage/staten/sophomores/
www.teach-nology.com/web_tools/
www.onestopenglish.com
www.oup.com/elt
www.cambridge.org/elt

Remember that as you browse through these sites, you might discover many more interesting ones. You could chat on matters related to teaching or learning English in www.kidlink.org or discuss with fellow students in www.eslcafe.com/discussion

You could even consult a grammar doctor to provide you a cure for your grammar maladies in www.englishclub.net/grammar/index.shtml

So happy *surfing!*